Know Your Customers !

How Customer Marketing Can Increase Profits

JAY CURRY

KOGAN PAGE

First published in 1991 in the Netherlands in Dutch by Management Press bv, Amsterdam, entitled *Customer Marketing*, ©Jay Curry 1991.

This edition first published in Great Britain in 1992 by Kogan Page Ltd.

Kogan Page Limited
120 Pentonville Road
London N1 9JN

Copies of the spreadsheets are available in Lotus 1-2-3 and Excel for personal computers operating on MS/DOS, and for the Apple Macintosh. For more information, contact: Jay Curry, MSP Associates, Oranje Nassaulaan 53, 1075 AK Amsterdam, The Netherlands; telephone 31-20-679-3077; Fax 31-20-679-2224

British Library Cataloguing in Publication Data

A CIP record for this book is available from the British Library.

ISBN 0-7494-0751-4 PB
ISBN 0-7494-0844-8 HB

Typeset by Saxon Printing Ltd, Derby
Printed and bound in Great Britain by Clays Ltd, St Ives plc

Contents

Preface

Do we need another 'marketing'?

It seems we are confronted every day with some new form of 'marketing': action marketing . . . interactive marketing . . . database marketing . . . relationship marketing . . . non-profit marketing . . . and so on.

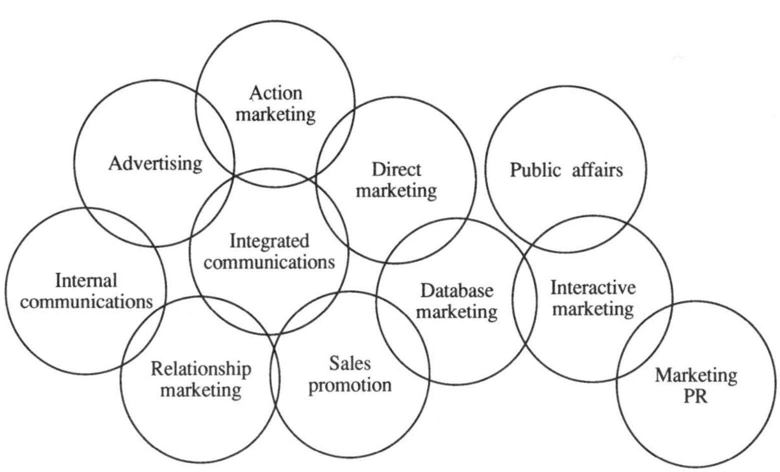

Figure 1

When you come down to it, most of these new 'marketings' have been invented by advertising and marketing services agencies trying to position their company uniquely.

And these 'marketings', based on a technique, technology or medium, are strongly pushed by the specialists in the technique, technology or medium.

If you want to increase sales, the sales promotion agency or department will tell you that sales promotion is the answer to a lot of problems. A direct mail specialist will generally recommend a mailing. And the PR man will suggest a 'media event' to generate press coverage.

It's simply human nature. The specialist earns his daily bread from his speciality – and doesn't feel comfortable outside it. In short, if the only tool you have is a hammer, every problem looks like a nail.

This kind of thinking often results in some smashed fingers: costly marketing and sales activities which don't work because they are based on inappropriate methods.

Isn't it about time to stop arguing about the kinds of technique or technology we use and concentrate on our marketing objectives?

Shouldn't the media and methods we use – and what we call them – be subordinate to our goals?

When you get down to it, companies are involved with only two kinds of goal-related 'marketing': corporate marketing and customer marketing.

Corporate marketing

Objective:

Convince people that the company is a worthy (potential) business partner.

Targets:

- **employees**
- **shareholders**
- **government**
- **trade colleagues**
- **customers, prospects, suspects**
- **etc.**

Media and methods:

Whatever are needed to reach the objective.

Customer marketing

Objective:

Identify, acquire, keep and develop customers.

Targets:

- **customers**
- **prospects**
- **suspects**

Media and methods:

Whatever are needed to reach the objective.

Figure 2 *Corporate versus customer marketing*

Corporate marketing has the goal of persuading different

groups that a company or organisation is a worthy business partner. The groups include customers and prospects, of course, but also other key groups such as shareholders, employees, legislators, government regulators, local government authorities, people living in the neighbourhood of the company, competitors and colleagues, suppliers, etc.

Customer marketing is focused solely on prospects and customers. The goal of customer marketing is to identify, create, keep and upgrade customers.

Since corporate marketing and customer marketing are goal related, the question of which media and methods they employ is totally irrelevant. Both corporate and customer marketers can use the techniques and technologies of direct marketing, sales promotion, PR, personal sales, or whatever.

For instance, a distributor of high-tech gear recently told me that he raised 'brand awareness' in his market sector from 0 to 40 per cent simply by sending mailings to his prospects and suspects. No full colour, two-page advertisements were needed for this successful corporate marketing campaign.

Corporate marketing is an essential activity for every business. So is customer marketing. And that's what this book is all about.

Acknowledgements

This book would not have been possible without the help and support of:

- the clients (customers!) which I have been honoured to serve – and learn from;
- my partners Wil Wurtz, for helping me juggle the critical success factors, and Maurice de Hond, for the concept of customer marketing ratings;
- the stars on the 'Direct Marketing Borscht Circuit' – Murray Raphel, Robert Liederman and Ray Considine – whose concepts, ideas and presentation styles have inspired me over the years;
- Ed McLean, the guy who got me into the business;
- Magi Steinberger, for her comments on the final copy; and
- Yolanda Curry-van Berge Henegouwen, who has had to put up with being a night-time 'computer widow' while this manuscript was in development.

Any faults or omissions are the sole responsibility of the author.

Amsterdam, February 1992

Part 1:

Introduction to Customer Marketing

Chapter 1

What Business Are You In?

Has a consultant ever asked you this simple but profound question? If so, he may have been trying to appear wise and all-knowing. But more likely he was trying to see if you are *product orientated* or *market orientated.*

If you answer the question, 'What business are you in?' in relation to your primary product or service:

We sell shoes.
We are accountants.
We build houses.

you probably are rather product orientated. And this can be dangerous.

As Theodore Levitt pointed out in his classic article 'Marketing Myopia', the presidents of American railway companies in the early 1900s, if asked, would have answered the question like this:

We are in the business of operating trains.

The result of this narrow, product-orientated thinking was that virtually every US rail company went bankrupt or faced serious problems because they missed out on the rapid growth of the airlines and the development of a sophisticated highway system as a way to get things and people from place A to place B.

For the railroads, a better answer would have been:

We are in the transportation business.

Another example is IBM. Thomas Watson, Jr, son of the IBM founder, tells in his recent book, *Father, Son & Co*, how IBM almost missed out on the computer revolution in the early 1950s. Many IBM-ers – including his forceful father – would have answered the question this way:

We are in the business of supplying punch card machinery.

The old-guard IBM-ers were making huge profits selling the machines which processed the cards carrying the famous 'Do not fold, spindle or mutilate' admonition. They simply refused to believe in the benefits of magnetic tape as a medium to store data, and computers to process that data. Watson Junior, hearing major customers complain about the costs of storing and managing millions of punch cards, realised just in time that IBM's answer to the question should be:

We are in the business of data processing.

By exploiting and developing computer technology as a better, faster and cheaper way to process data, IBM became one of the largest and most successful companies in the world. (And converted from magnetic tape to hard disk technology when it became more cost-effective as a storage medium.)

As these examples indicate, a market orientation is much healthier for you and your business in this fast-changing world. But this book proposes that you deepen your market orientation to the level where it all happens: *the customer*.

Your company's revenues, profits and market share – and your salary – come ultimately from only one source: *your customers*!

No matter what products and services you provide, be it bars of chocolate, computers, insurance or temporary staff – customers are the heart of your business. When you get right down to it, the one single thing a company needs to be in business is a customer:

- You don't need money to be in business.
- You don't need to have an idea to be in business.
- You don't need a shop, factory or office location to be in business.
- You don't need personnel to be in business.
- You don't even need a product or service to be in business.

All these things help, of course. But without a customer, you're not in business. If you have just one customer, you are in business. If you have a lot of *good customers*, you have a successful business. If your company is successful – and I hope it is – I'm willing to bet you have developed a solid base of good customers who do nice things like this:

- *Buy more from you – even if your prices are (somewhat) higher than the competition.*
  Obviously you can't swindle people and expect to get away with it. But think about that small grocery shop or clothes boutique where they know your name or the service is pleasant. Yes, you pay a bit more. But you keep coming back.
- *Recommend you to colleagues, family, friends.*
  There's no better promotional message than a recommendation from a satisfied customer. People talk about their experiences with suppliers, both good and bad. A recent study showed that data processing (DP) managers rate advice from colleagues as one of the most important sources of information for buying a system, and that more than 60 per cent of DP managers give advice privately to colleagues outside their own organisation!

  Imagine – the DP manager of Procter & Gamble meets the DP manager of Unilever at a computer conference. They don't talk about soap. They talk about who's doing what to whom in the DP community – and their experiences, good and bad, with suppliers.

  While a good customer will generate a lot of business for you, a dissatisfied customer can hurt you badly. Who was it who said: 'For every complaint there are ten other dissatisfied customers who didn't make the effort to tell you of their dissatisfaction? And since every dissatisfied customer gripes to an average of six people, every complaint represents 60 people who are walking around with a negative image of your company.'
- *Make you the 'standard' for the organisation or family.*
  What could be better than having the boss at your customer site sending out a memo to all employees: 'All (name your product or service) must be ordered from (the name of your company)!' Good customers write memos like that.
- *Try out your new products and help you to make them better.*
  Good customers are usually willing to invest their time and effort to help you develop and improve your (new) products and services. In the case of mainframe computers and sophisticated technology, customer involvement in

research and development of new products can be worth tens of thousands of pounds or more in man-hours and expertise. And the best part is this: *as customers become involved in your business, they tend to become better customers!*

- *Use your support, service and other facilities.*
  Service, support, training, add-ons. These often highly profitable products and services are usually offered to customers with whom you have a good relationship.

If you believe that good customers are so essential to your business, you can answer the question 'What business are you in?' with:

> 'We are in the business of developing a solid base of *good customers* for our products and services.'

Know Your Customers!

Erratum

The illustration on page 31 should appear as follows:

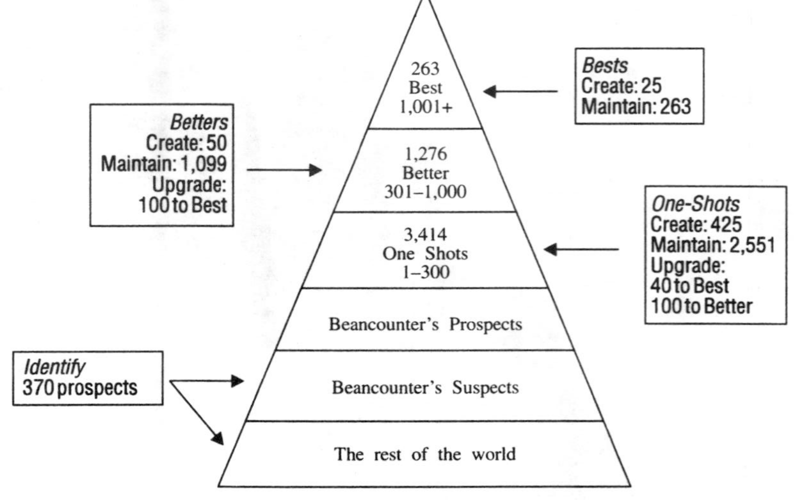

Figure 9 *Beancounter's customer goals*

Chapter 2

The Customer Pyramid

If having a lot of (good) customers is the key to business success, you will want to know how many of what kinds of customer you really have. One way to find out is to construct a 'customer pyramid' like this:

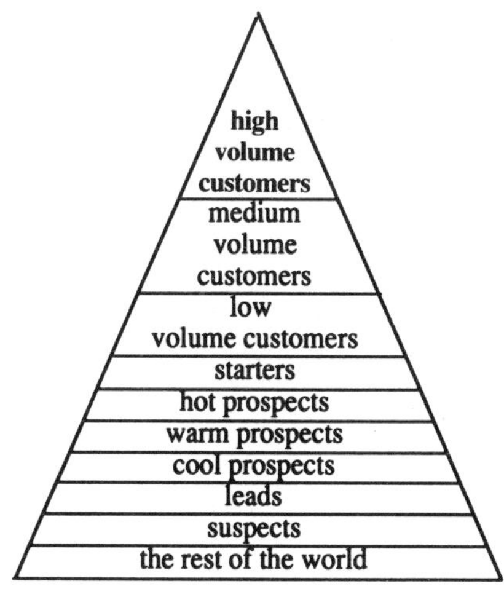

Figure 3 *The customer pyramid*

Take a list of your customers and rank them by turnover. Chances are you will discover that you have a customer base consisting of:

- a small number of *high volume customers* who give you a lot of business;
- a larger number of *medium volume customers;* and
- many more *low volume customers* who do business with you only once in a while, or at a low purchasing level;
- a number of *starters*, new customers, who may or may not turn out to be good ones.

Your customer pyramid may also contain prospects – people and companies with whom you are in contact, but they are not yet buyers. These prospects can be segmented into:

- *hot prospects* – people who are ready to buy, and you are on the short list.
- *warm prospects* – people who will probably buy in the short term, and you have a reasonable chance of getting the business.
- *cold prospects* – people who you are in touch with, but who are not ready to buy, or they have indicated that they are not happy about doing business with you.
- *leads* – responses from marketing activities which have not yet been qualified as one type of prospect or another.

To round off the customer pyramid, you may want to include the *suspects* in your market segment: people or companies who are likely to have a need for your products and services, but with whom you have as yet no relationship.

After that comes the rest of the world (where some suspects might also be lurking).

After completing this exercise, you may well discover the validity of the old 80/20 rule which says that 80 per cent of your sales (and profits) come from 20 per cent of the people you do business with – your good customers.

How can you get more (good) customers? That's what customer marketing is all about.

Chapter 3

Customer Marketing Defined

Simply stated, the customer marketing process involves:

1. Getting suspects into your customer pyramid;
2. Qualifying promising prospects;
3. Converting them into customers; and then . . .
4. Moving them up the pyramid!

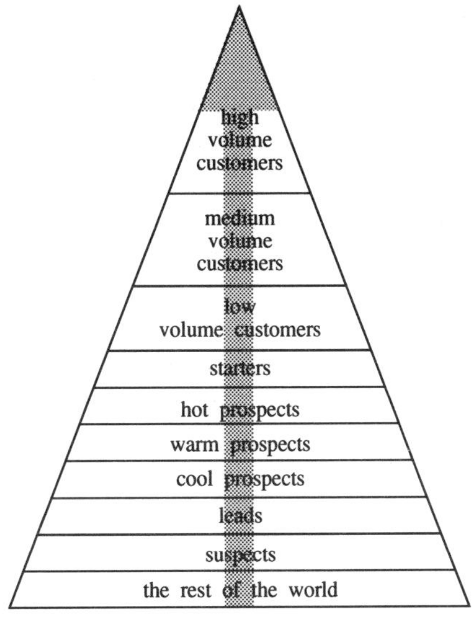

Figure 4 *The customer marketing process*

The result will be that you have more good customers. And, as we will see, the upward migration in your customer pyramid can give you explosive growth in profits – and increased customer satisfaction.

But to make it happen, you will need to use a solid base of information about your customers and prospects and a variety of methods and media.

Here is the 'official' definition of customer marketing:

> Customer marketing is a *planned process* which uses a *customer database* and an *integrated mix of methods and media* to meet *measurable customer goals*.

The second part of this book covers the customer marketing process in detail. For now, let's look deeper into the other three elements of customer marketing:

1. Customer database
2. Integrated mix of methods and media
3. Measurable customer goals.

Chapter 4

The Customer Database

Customer marketing requires your company to be highly customer orientated. But a customer orientation is only possible if you have a lot of information about your customers and can communicate with them personally.

Let's see how a customer orientated shopkeeper uses customer information to improve his business.

Consider Mr Jones, a chemist in a small town. He knows a lot about his customers and prospects, having lived and worked in the town for years. And he has a sophisticated customer database system – right between his ears.

When Mrs Smith walks in, Mr Jones plonks down a prepared prescription and says, 'Good morning, Mrs Smith. Your monthly prescription is here waiting for you.'

'Thank you, Mr Jones,' replies Mrs Smith.

Mr Jones scans the Smith file in his customer database and retrieves some data.

'How is your husband's hip? Is it any better?' asks Mr Jones.

'Why, thank you for asking,' Mrs Smith responds. 'It's better, but not 100 per cent.'

Mr Jones pulls a box off the shelf and hands it to Mrs Smith. 'Why don't you try this out, Mrs Smith? We just got it in. A 16-valve, turbo-power hot water bottle. Costs just £19.99. It's supposed to work wonders. But if it doesn't, you just bring it back for a refund.'

'I'll just do that,' says Mrs Smith. 'Thank you very much.'

'You're welcome. Have a nice day,' replies Mr Jones, putting the money in his cash register – £19.99 in extra turnover.

Here is a classic case of upgrading a regular customer through use of information about that customer.

Of course, you can rely on your own memory if your customers are few and you have frequent and personal contact with them. But what if you have thousands of customers, and you don't meet them personally? The answer to this problem: your customer database.

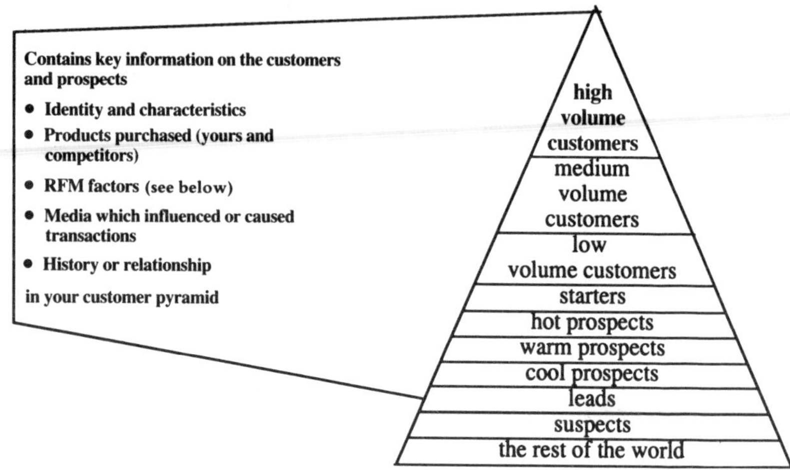

Figure 5 *The customer database*

Mail order companies, publishers, credit card vendors and other sophisticated direct marketers pioneered the development of customer databases running on large, expensive mainframe computers in the 1960s and 1970s.

Today, for less than £5,000 you can buy a computer and database package capable of storing and managing information on tens of thousands of customers such as:

- *Customer identity and characteristics.*
  Basic data such as names, addresses, telephone numbers are a must, but also characteristics such as type of business, number of employees, etc (for business) and sex, date of birth, family size, etc (for consumers).
- *Products purchased/requests/interests.*
  It is also important to store information on the products and services purchased or enquired about. From this information, you can deduce interest areas if you haven't already asked these via surveys or other means.
- *RFM factors.*
  Recency = when customer last bought.
  Frequency = how often they bought in, say, the past year.
  Monetary = how much they spent.

The concept of RFM factors was developed by mail order companies to segment their customer types. But the basic principle can be useful for all customer marketers.

- *Media and/or activity which influenced transaction.*
  You'll want to know which medium – be it a sales visit or a response advertisement – led to a sale or brought you the customer in the first place.
- *A history of the customer relationship.*
  If you get it right, your database will contain a complete history of your relationship with each customer and prospect in your customer pyramid.

Once you have this kind of information about your customers, you can also communicate with them on a *personal* basis with one goal in mind:

> To create a strong link with your customers, just like the old-fashioned shopkeepers used to do, even if you have 1,000, 10,000, 100,000, 1,000,000 customers or more.

Imagine, for example, that you own a clothes shop and you have thousands of customers registered in your database. An analysis reveals that there are two types of women who buy baby clothes:

Type A: women aged 59–99
Type B: women aged 19–39

You use your brilliant mind to determine that Type A women are probably grandmothers or aunt types; Type B women are probably mothers.

Around 1 December you send a high-quality mailing featuring expensive and exclusive children's clothes to the Type A women, with a signed, 'personal' letter which comments that they have bought children's clothes in the past, and offers the collection as gift ideas.

'Thank you for thinking of me', say the Type A women, reaching for their cheque books while heading out of the door to visit your shop.

After the Christmas rush, you see what children's clothes are left over. You feature these items in an inexpensive mailing sent to Type B women as a post-Christmas sale of fine clothes at reduced prices.

'Thank you for thinking of me', say the Type B women, reaching for their cheque books, smiling secretly at the fact that they can buy the same items as their mothers-in-law a few weeks before – but at a 30 per cent discount!

Customer marketing makes people happy. Especially those who practise it.

And the same principles apply whether you're selling bulldozers or baby clothes. But it will only work if you have collected information about your customers and prospects in your customer database, and can manage and manipulate the information efficiently.

An additional benefit of the customer database is accountability for marketing and sales expenses.

Who was it who said: 'We know that 50 per cent of all advertising expenditure is pure waste – but we don't know which 50 per cent'?

This kind of thinking is totally unacceptable to customer marketers.

If you record all transactions in your customer database, including the medium which stimulated that transaction, you should get a clear idea of how much value you received for all advertising and sales money spent.

Chapter 5

An Integrated Mix of Methods and Media

You hear and read much about 'integrated communications' these days. Usually that means some form of close coordination of a promotional campaign which combines advertising, direct marketing, sales promotion and publicity.

Customer marketing calls for the planning, registration and evaluation of *all contacts* between the company and its customers, prospects and suspects whatever the method or media: a sales visit, a direct mail shot, a response advertisement, or whatever.

The purpose of this integrated approach is to ensure that the most cost-effective medium and method can be employed for each customer or prospect situation.

As an example, let's say you are trying to get new customers for your fax machines. You can use your sales force to phone companies to find out if they have a fax; identify the decision maker; try to get a sales appointment; make the sales call; and close the deal.

You'll make some sales, of course. But given the high cost of a salesperson, and the limited amount of time a salesperson has (only 1,400 selling hours per year!), you will probably find that this mix of media and methods delivers more new customers, more sales and at a lower cost per sale:

- *Outbound telemarketing* to see if the suspect company has a fax; identify fax decision maker;
- *Direct mail* to the fax decision makers to generate sales leads;
- *Internal sales force call* to qualify the leads and make appointments for a demonstration;
- *External sales force* gives the demonstration, creates the customer, closes the sale;
- *Outbound telemarketing* to non-respondents; make appointment for a demonstration.

In the case of current customers, you can substitute some routine sales visits (costing £75 each) to regular customers with programmed telephone calls (business calls) from the sales force (costing £5 each). The customer will appreciate the service, while the cost of the customer contact is reduced by £70. If the customer places an order over the telephone – which happens more often than you may think – the cost of the sale is a mere £5!

You can use virtually every kind of medium and method with customer marketing. But you may get yourself lost in a semantic jungle trying to distinguish between 'above-the-line' and 'below-the-line' media and joining the never-ending debates about the real meaning of 'direct marketing', 'sales promotion', 'advertising', 'marketing PR' and 'interactive marketing'.

To make life simple for yourself, categorise your selling methods and media into their degree of personalisation, like this:

- *Personal media and methods.*
  These involve two or more people communicating with each other who are – or become – personally acquainted.
- *Semi-personal media.*
  These involve an identified company representative who contacts a prospect or customer by name in the hope of eliciting a response which will develop into a (sales) dialogue.
- *Non-personal media.*
  These involve a message distributed widely to no specific individuals (suspects) in the hope that interested persons (prospects) will identify themselves by responding, thus leading to a sales dialogue.

As Figure 6 indicates, the more personal a medium is, the more effective it is – and expensive in terms of cost per contact.

A more detailed description of these methods and media can be found on pages 72–5 in Step 6. Select Methods and Media.

The integration of media and methods targeted on customers and prospects requires close coordination among the people involved and in charge of them.

- The *sales manager*, of course, runs the external and internal sales forces, and often has some control over the service staff, and telemarketing.
- The *marketing manager* usually controls the budget and activities for direct mail, advertising and promotions, and often telemarketing as well.

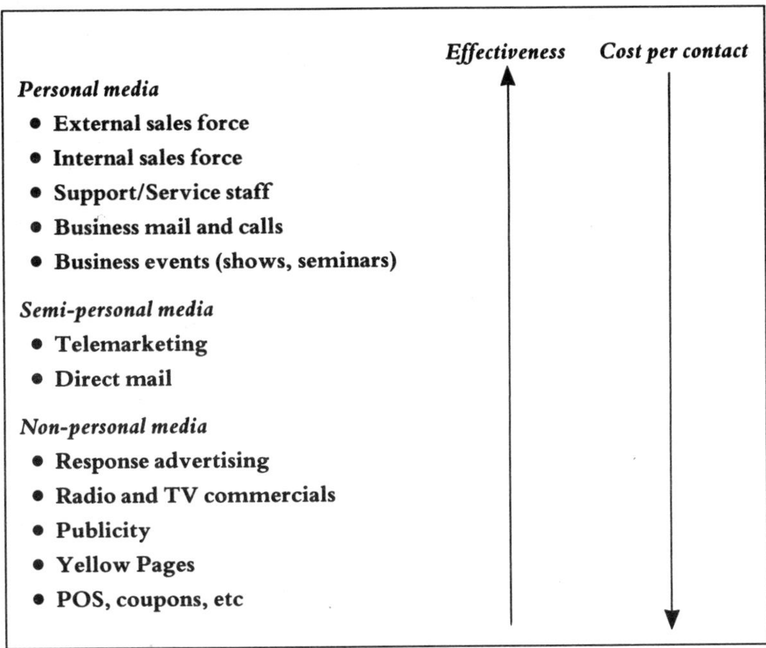

Figure 6 *Customer marketing methods and media*

Thus customer marketing involves some kind of integration – formally or informally – of the sales and marketing function. (It's not always easy to accomplish . . .)

Chapter 6

Customer Goals

What goals do you set for your company or business unit for a planning period? Market share? Profits? Profits as a percentage of sales? Turnover? Return on investment?

These are all tried and true managerial goals. And customer marketing does not neglect them.

But customer marketing recognises the inescapable fact of life that market share, profits, sales and return on investment come from only one source: *customers*.

Thus customer marketing requires you to translate your normal goals into *customer goals*, and specify how many of what kinds of customer you want to:

- identify (get prospects, leads)
- acquire (make a new customer)
- keep (maintain purchasing pattern)
- upgrade (increase purchasing)

for a given planning period.

Let's see how customer goal setting works in practice at Beancounter Publishing Ltd, a publisher of loose-leaf information services for accountants and financial managers. (*Note*. This example is based on real world data from an existing publishing company.)

Here are the basic figures for Beancounter Publishing Ltd.

Turnover	1,559,154
Cost of product	559,704
Gross margin	999,450
Total marketing sales	450,000
Contribution	549,450
Overheads	400,000
Pre-tax profit	149,450
Number of customers	4,953
Number of subscriptions	7,194
Turnover per customer	315
Subscriptions per customer	1.45

The staff at Beancounter decided to make a customer pyramid. It cost a few days with the computer, but here is what Beancounter Publishing discovered:

- 263 'Best' customers are good for £386,610 in sales, buying an average of 4.75 subscriptions providing an average £1,402 per customer in revenues.
- 1,276 'Better' customers deliver £719,957 in sales (average revenue £564, average subscriptions just under 2).
- 3,414 'One-Shot' customers – the great majority – subscribe to only one publication and deliver £510,587 in sales from an average revenue per customer of £150.

The staff at Beancounter made this customer pyramid based on this information:

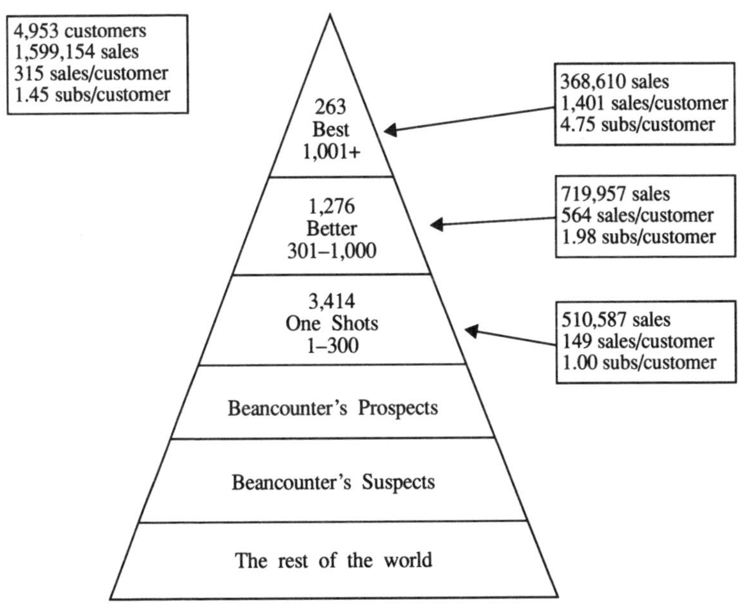

Figure 7 *Beancounter's customers*

And as the chart shows, 31 per cent of Beancounter's customers – the 'Best' and 'Betters' – are good for 68 per cent of Beancounter's turnover.

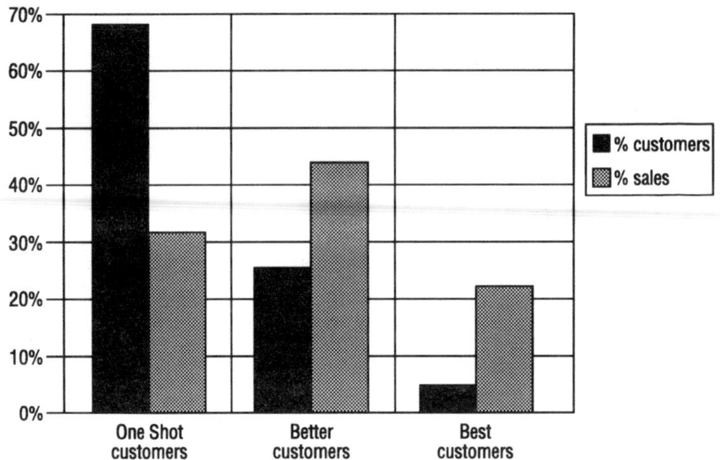

Figure 8 *Beancounter's customers and turnover*

Thus the bad news for Beancounter is that it has few customers with a high turnover, and many customers with a low turnover.

But that was also the good news! Beancounter has a working business relationship with a large number of customers. And from the Beancounter customer database, it can be seen who these customers are, what they buy, what they don't buy, what they should buy.

By reviewing spending patterns and discussing customer potential with the sales force, the customer goals for Beancounter Publishing Ltd were set as follows:

- *Upgrade* 400 'One-Shot' customers to 'Better' status and 40 to 'Best' status; 100 'Better' customers to 'Best' status.
- *Acquire* 500 customers (425 'One-Shots', 50 'Betters' and 25 'Best') from the pool of prospects and suspects to replace an expected natural drop-off from the customer base.
- *Keep* 3,913 customers (2,551 'One-Shots'; 1,099 'Betters' and all 263 'Bests') who are not candidates for upgrading, and not expected to fall away naturally owing to going out of business, dissatisfaction, mergers, etc.
- *Identify* 370 new prospects from the pool of suspects.

To make these goals clear throughout the company, the manager of Beancounter distributed this chart to all marketing, sales and editorial people:

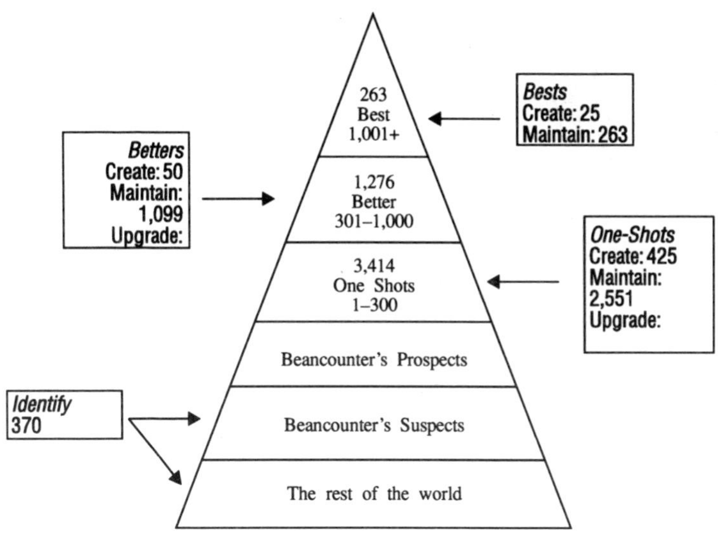

Figure 9 *Beancounter's customer goals*

What is the profit pay-off for Beancounter if its customer goals are achieved? The next chapter makes that clear.

Chapter 7

Customer Marketing: The Profit Pay-Off

Customer marketing seeks to create an upward migration in your customer pyramid. The result should be not just an increase in turnover, but an explosive profit growth.

For example, here is what Beancounter's customer pyramid looks like after meeting its customer goals:

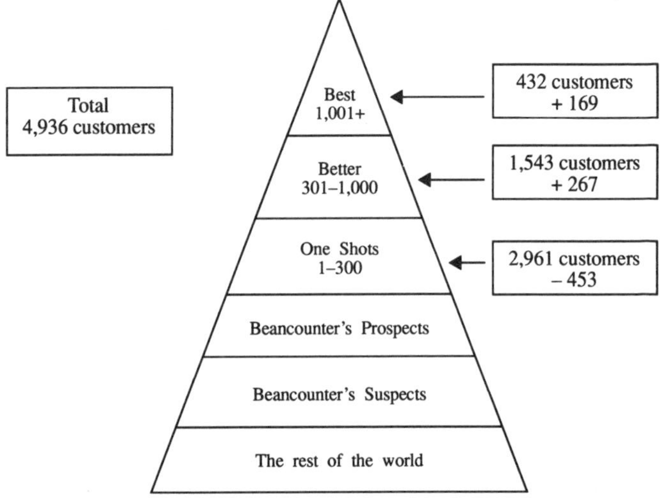

Figure 10 *Beancounter's customer pyramid after customer marketing*

Here we see the enhancement of the customer base by customer marketing:

- an increase of 169 'Best' customers
- an increase of 267 'Better' customers
- a decrease of 453 'One-Shot' customers.

More important, though, is the 'bottom line' impact on Beancounter Publishing Ltd. The chart shows it – a whopping 118 per cent profit increase – *despite a slight decrease (−17) in the total number of customers*!

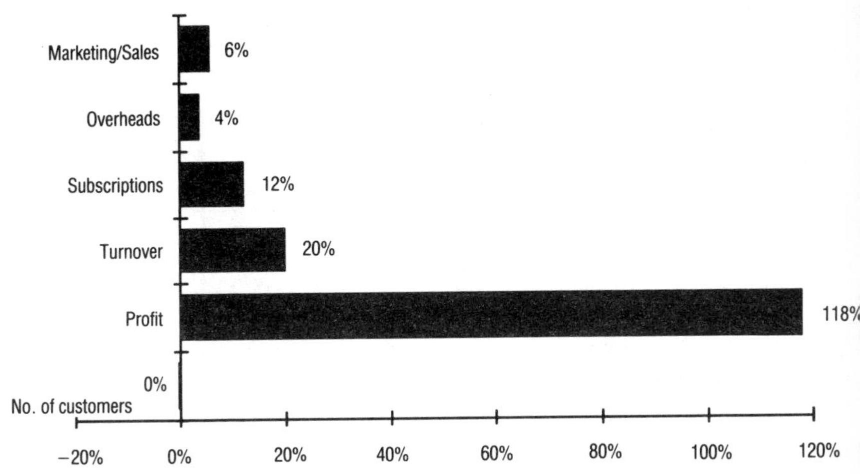

Figure 11 *Customer marketing: the profit for Beancounter*

How were these profits possible? Because the customer marketing profit pay-off is based on two facts of life.

> *Fact of life number 1. It takes much less time, effort and money to sell to your existing customers than to prospects and suspects who are not yet your customers.*

Take the personal computer business, for example. You have to work hard to make your first sale to a doubting prospect. It takes time – maybe three meetings and two demonstrations – to convince him that you understand what he's looking for . . . that you have the know-how and service capability in house to help him out when the system goes down . . . that you won't go out of business tomorrow. And all that time you spend with him costs money.

But once you've got him as a good customer, the second and subsequent systems purchases may require no more effort than accepting his telephone order.

Customer marketing profits are well known to book club operations. You've seen the advertisements: three books for only £5! It can cost a book club from £15 to £50 to get a starter, or new customer. But the following sales contact, via catalogues and mailings, cost only about £1 each. And assuming the member buys four times a year with an average purchase of £10 the profit is very interesting indeed!

Customer financials: Book club example

	First year	Subsequent years
Revenue	45.00	40.00
Product cost	11.25	10.00
Premium cost	5.00	0.00
Marketing cost	55.00	4.00
Total marketing sales costs	60.00	4.00
Total costs	71.25	14.00
Gross profit	– 26.25	26.00
Marketing ROI*	– 44%	650%

*Marketing ROI = Profit divided by all marketing and sales costs (investment).

Fact of life number 2. Good customers are more profitable than other customers.

The 'average' airline customer flies maybe twice a year to visit the folks at home. But 'average' can be the most dangerous word in business. My brother Ren, the rocket scientist, pointed out that if you add up all the people in your city, and make certain statistically valid calculations, you can come to the conclusion that the 'average' citizen has one breast and one testicle!

There are fewer than a million flyers in the USA who deliver more than 70 per cent of the profits for the whole air transportation industry: business people who fly frequently – and first class.

That's why almost every airline has a 'frequent flyer' programme to identify, create, keep and upgrade these highly profitable companies.

To summarise, customer marketing delivers profits because it puts your focus:

- on current customers, and thus reduced selling costs;
- on upgrading 'average' customers to good customers who are more profitable.

Figure 12 tells the story.

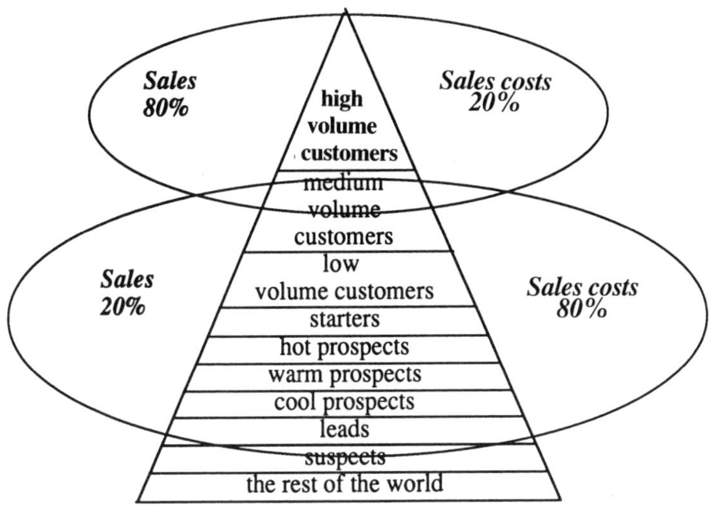

Figure 12 *Customer marketing: the profit pay-off*

Customer satisfaction: the extra profit of customer marketing

A second benefit of customer marketing is that it can stimulate – yes, even force – your employees to focus on your customers and satisfy their needs.

When you set customer goals, measure customer results and reward people based on these results, you can achieve more than any other kind of 'customer care' or 'quality circle' programmes.

Take the case of a bank branch office. The manager is usually evaluated and rewarded based on the total amount of deposits, loans and other sales. The other employees are usually rewarded on the basis of relatively subjective evaluations – and their customer service often suffers as a result, creating the need for 'quality training'.

But what if the bank manager and employees know that they will be rewarded by an increase in the quality and quantity of their customer pyramid?

You can be sure that the manager will focus his own and his staff's efforts on identifying, creating and maintaining customers. And there will be a definite improvement in customer service, because a lost customer means less reward.

We have reached the end of our introduction to customer marketing. In subsequent chapters you will learn more about the customer marketing process, and how you might implement it in your business.

Part 2:

Ten Steps to Make Customer Marketing Work for You

Earlier in this book we defined customer marketing like this: Customer marketing is a *planned process* which uses a *customer database* and an *integrated mix of methods and media* to meet *measurable customer goals*.

We discussed customer goals, the customer database, and an integrated mix of media and methods.

Finally, we demonstrated the profit pay-off of customer marketing in terms of real money and increased customer satisfaction.

Could customer marketing play a role in your business? If you think so, or want to know more, this section describes the customer marketing process in detail.

You will learn a ten-step programme to introduce customer marketing in your organisation regardless of size. (*Note*. If yours is a medium or large company, I strongly urge you to begin customer marketing in one small business unit. Try it out on a small scale at first. You will make some mistakes and learn some valuable lessons before making any attempt to implement the process on a company-wide basis.)

To illustrate and demonstrate the customer marketing process, we will use a case: International Widgets Ltd (InterWidget). Although InterWidget is an industrial company with an external sales force, the basic customer marketing strategies and tactics used by InterWidget can also be applied by all kinds of business, including retail, financial services and even fast-moving consumer goods.

Customer marketing case: International Widgets Ltd

International Widgets Ltd (InterWidget) is a maker of high-grade widgets used in the machine tool industry. Here are its financial results last year:

InterWidget financial results last year

Turnover	3,642,544
Cost of product	1,827,571
Gross margin	1,814,973
Sales costs	601,950
Marketing costs	396,616
Total marketing sales	998,566
Contribution	816,407
Overheads	596,297
Pre-tax profit	220,110
Number of customers	866
Turnover per customer	4,207
Pre-tax profit per customer	254

InterWidget is not a world-beater, but at least it is showing a profit. Seeking to raise InterWidget's pre-tax profits to 10 per cent of sales, Bill de Vries, InterWidget's President, included these items in his business plan:

- increase sales by 10 per cent by recruiting 100 new customers
- hire another salesperson (+ £60,000)
- increase marketing budget (+ £40,000)
- keep overheads the same.

Achieving the business plan would produce the following financials for InterWidget:

InterWidget budget next year (traditional)

Turnover	4,000,000
Cost of product	2,000,000
Gross margin	2,000,000
Marketing/Sales:salespeople	660,000
Marketing/Sales: other	440,000
Total marketing sales	1,100,000
Contribution	900,000
Overheads	600,000
Pre-tax profit	300,000
Number of customers	966
Turnover per customer	4,141
Pre-tax profit per customer	311

But Bill de Vries discarded this plan. It would not result in the dramatic improvements he learned could be achieved by customer marketing, and he was uneasy about the investment needed in new sales people. So he decided to follow the ten-step customer marketing process.

Step 1

Capture Customer Data

Customer marketing makes effective use of information about your customers and prospects. So your first step is to pull together all the information on your prospects and customers which you have on hand.

You want to know who your customers are, their characteristics, what they buy from you, when they buy, how much they buy.

Even if you don't have a customer database up and running, you will discover you have in your organisation more data than you thought. Think about these sources:

- invoices
- contract files
- order forms
- service files
- credit applications/cards
- warranty and guarantees
- sales force reports
- general correspondence.

When you have exhausted your internal resources, you have to go outside to gather more information.

What is the best way to find out about your customers and prospects? The answer to this question is quite simple: *you ask them*!

It is amazing how much information customers and prospects are prepared to give you – if you just ask them politely, and provide a reward. Believe it or not, 70 per cent of all the people we asked agreed to spend half an hour with us on the telephone to answer all kinds of questions about their office equipment. Why? Because we showed an interest in them – and offered a free dinner, with a chance of a week's holiday as the grand prize. (The dinner didn't cost *us* anything either – the deal from the restaurant was one dinner free if one was paid for!)

Capturing customer data – the InterWidget case

It took InterWidget about two days of looking through the financial department's computer to come up with the names of customers and their purchasing patterns. But they still didn't know much more about the customers than their names.

To fill up their customer database, InterWidget conducted a postal customer satisfaction survey (with telephone calls to non-respondents) which asked customers to air any complaints and provide advice as to how InterWidget could improve their products and services. The survey ended with requests for information about the respondent's company, such as number of employees, turnover category, etc. It worked like a charm!

Step 2

Make Your Customer Pyramid

Once you have basic customer/prospect data you can define and quantify exactly what a customer or prospect is – and is not – and how to construct your customer pyramid.

Customer types by turnover

The simplest – and most used – method to define customers is simply by sales or turnover. Make a list of your customers during the last year, ranked by turnover in descending order. Then break out the top 5 per cent as the 'high' customers; the next 15 per cent of customers as the 'medium' customers; and the remaining 80 per cent as the 'low' customers. After that you add up the turnover per category and look at the results.

More often than not, you will discover that the top 20 per cent of your customers deliver about 80 per cent of your turnover.

You may also want to add a 'super' tier of customers by breaking out the top 1 per cent of your customers to see what they deliver. And here you may find out to your shock and surprise that a handful of customers may represent 25 per cent of your turnover – or more!

Customer types by RFM factors

Another variation is to define your customers by RFM factors:

- Recency – when did someone last purchase?
- Frequency – how often have they purchased within the past year?
- Monetary – how much did the customer spend?

For instance, a clothing retailer determined that the average family spends £2,000 a year on clothing and visits clothes shops eight times a year. He then defined his customers as follows:

	Recency (last visit)	*Frequency* (visits per year)	*Monetary* (yearly sales)
'Good'	within 3 months	four	£1,000
'Average'	within 6 months	two	£400
'Casual'	within 9 months	one	£100
'Starter'	within 1 month	?	?

Customer types by product purchases

You can also define types of customer by products or services purchased. For instance, in the insurance business, customers are often categorised as 'life' and 'casualty' clients.

Customer types by repeat purchases

If you produce capital goods such as large machines and cars, a more relevant way to define customers is by repeat purchases. For example, your 'top' customers have purchased a car three or more times in a row; a 'good' customer has purchased two in a row; and a 'starter' customer has bought a car from you for the first time.

Prospect types

A prospect is a person or company with whom you are in some form of dialogue or contact, and who is qualified to purchase your product or service: they have the money and the need.

It is also necessary to define and quantify your prospects in terms of probability that they will become customers, when and the amount of their order. It is only with this information that you can make reasonable business projections.

Most companies rate prospects using a three-tier system, such as A, B and C prospects. I have a personal preference for temperature – hot, warm and cool – to rate prospects something like this:

- hot prospect: 70 per cent chance of order and/or decision within 30 days.
- warm prospect: 50 per cent chance of order and/or decision within 90 days.
- cool prospect: less than 50 per cent chance of order and/or decision more than 90 days away.

Suspects

Some marketers also use the concept of a suspect. A suspect is a person or company which has all the earmarks of a customer or prospect, but you haven't yet made personal contact to evaluate their real need for your product and service, their ability to pay – and the chances that they will be doing any business with you.

Having analysed and defined your customers and prospects, you can now make your own customer pyramid.

Customer pyramid – the InterWidget case

After some experimentation, Bill de Vries segmented InterWidget's customer base into these customer types:

- Topper customers: purchase more than £10,000 per year
- Good Guy customers: purchase £3,000–£10,000 per year
- Low Boy customers: purchase £1–£2,999 per year
- Prospects: companies which had requested information or had been visited by a salesperson, but have not yet ordered anything from InterWidget
- Suspects: machine tool companies in InterWidget's territory with whom InterWidget has no relationship of any kind – yet

and made this customer pyramid for InterWidget.

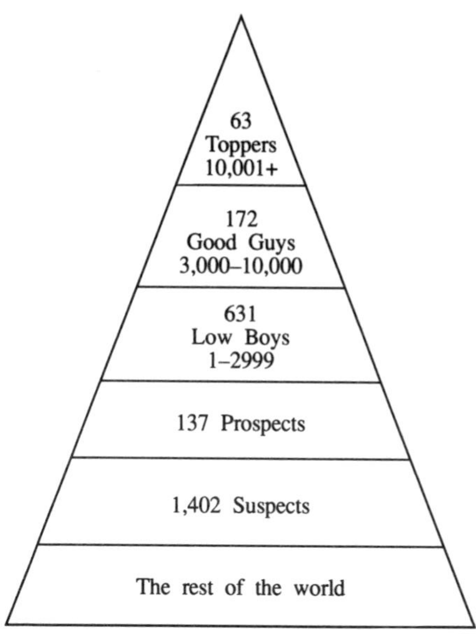

Figure 13 *InterWidget's customer pyramid*

Step 3

Analyse Your Customers

Now you have to build on the basic data used to make the customer pyramid and make a *financial analysis* and *market analysis* for each customer type.

Financial analysis

To understand what each type of customer means for your business, you have to get key financial data, such as:

- Sales: turnover after any commissions or discounts
- Gross margin: sales less direct cost of product
- Sales costs: costs of external and internal sales force
- Marketing costs: costs of semi- and non-personal media
- Contribution: gross margin less marketing and sales costs
- Overheads: all other indirect costs
- Pre-tax profit: speaks for itself!
- Sales per customer: average turnover per customer
- Customer profit: how much profit should be delivered by each (type) of customer
- Customer break-even: number of customers of each type needed to break even
- Return on marketing investment: what contribution was generated by the marketing and sales spend – including cost of personal media.

Take a careful look at the InterWidget financial data contained in the spreadsheets on pages 90–103 to see how you might structure your own financial information.

Once you have your financial data per customer type, you can make a more accurate budget and sharpen your financial planning to match spending efforts and activities to meet customer goals.

Market analysis

A market analysis of your customers – per type – should have two key kinds of information:

- *Customer share.* Customer share is the percentage of companies or consumers in your market (segment) with whom you do business. In addition to knowing where you stand versus competition, customer share data can help you to determine customer acquisition goals.
- *Customer characteristics.* Knowing the characteristics of each type of customer will help you to determine which customers are ripe for upgrading, and identify prospects and suspects you should target for customer acquisition efforts.

  In the business-to-business marketplace, common characteristics are type of industry, number of employees, total revenues. Other characteristics to look for in your customer base, depending on your business, may be very narrow or specific. For example, if you are selling training courses, your good customers will probably have a large training department and/or a training manager on the payroll.

  Consumer customers are often segmented by sex, age, house location, income level, education level, number of children, possession of one or more credit cards, etc.

Customer analysis – the InterWidget case

InterWidget financial analysis

Bill de Vries spent some long hours working on his spreadsheet, talking with the accountants and making some inspired assumptions. (For instance, he allocated marketing, sales and overheads equally across the prospect and customer groups because there was no way to do it differently.)

Copies of Bill's spreadsheets can be found on pages 90–103. They give you the details and show you how he set them up.

The first thing Bill de Vries discovered was that InterWidget was not immune from the 80/20 rule (80 per cent of turnover comes from 20 per cent of the customers). His Topper and Good Guy customers, 27 per cent of his customer base, were good for 74 per cent of the sales. Even more dramatic, these 235 customers contributed 94 per cent of InterWidget's profits!

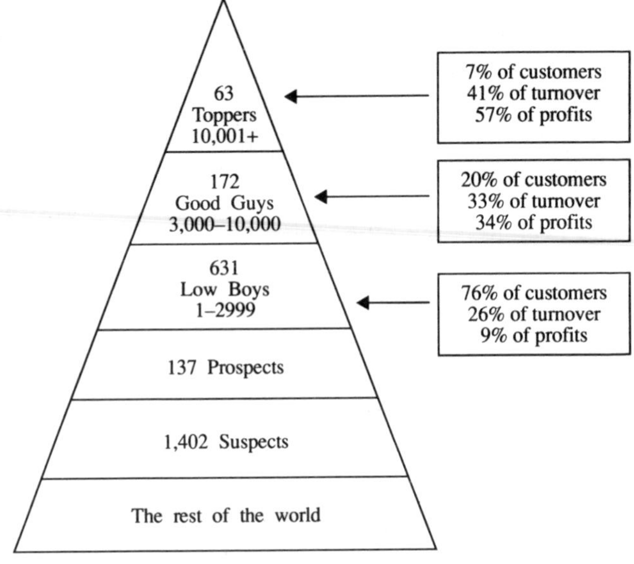

Figure 14 *The 80/20 rule at InterWidget*

Bill took a closer look at the numbers to find out why. And he discovered a major difference in return on sales and marketing return on investment for each customer type. As Figure 15 shows, the Low Boys delivered a 6 per cent return on sales versus 17 per cent on the Good Guys and a very nice 24 per cent for the Toppers.

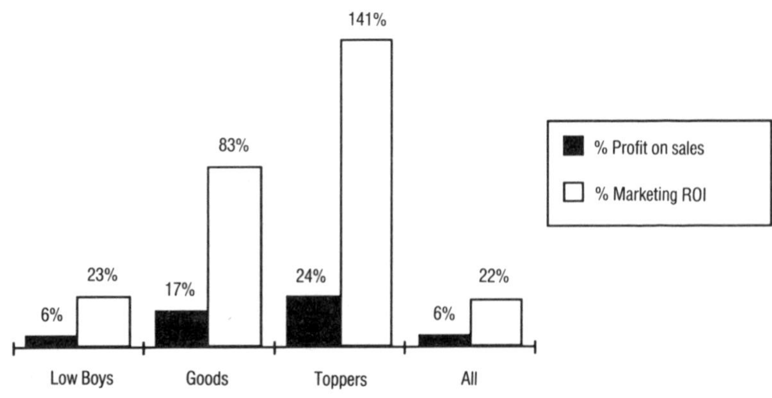

Figure 15 *InterWidget percentage profit and percentage ROI*

The difference in marketing ROI was understandable for Bill. But he was puzzled by the return on sales figures because InterWidget was doing about 6 per cent profit on return on sales for all customers. Why wasn't he getting a better return on sales?

Bill found the answer in his analysis of turnover and profit per customer type, as shown in Figure 16.

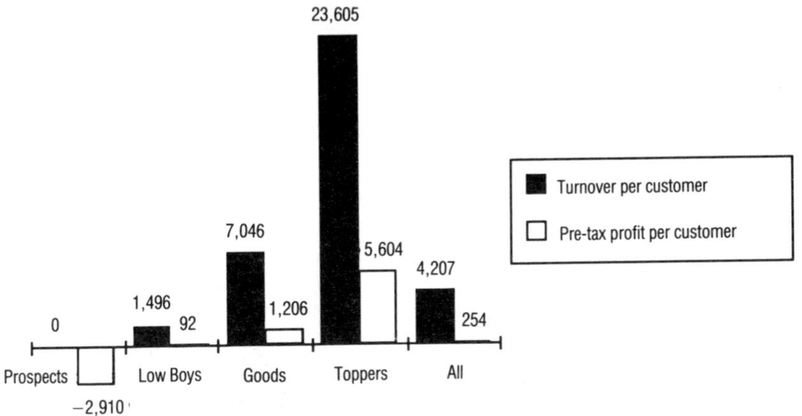

Figure 16 *InterWidget turnover and profit per customer type*

Here you see what Bill found out about the financial performance of his various customer types:

- 63 Toppers averaged £23,605 in turnover and £5,604 profit per customer.
- 172 Good Guys delivered an average of £7,046 in turnover and £1,206 profit per customer.
- 631 Low Boys – the great majority – were good for £1,496 in turnover each, with just £92 in profit per customer.

Most disturbing, however, was the fact that 137 prospects, with no turnover, were costing InterWidget £2,910 each in marketing and sales costs, plus overheads – a total of almost £400,000. The losses in the prospect category were cutting deeply into profits and overall return on sales.

Bill realised that he should be more careful about his marketing expenses on non-customers (prospects and suspects), and perhaps focus a bit more on the InterWidget customer base.

Above all, he concluded that InterWidget needed a lot more Topper customers. To find out where to get them, he carried out his market analysis.

InterWidget market analysis

Bill first made an analysis of his customer base to determine the characteristics of his customers based on the information InterWidget collected with the customer satisfaction survey. They key characteristic he focused on was the size of customers expressed in number of employees.

As Figure 17 shows, slightly more than half of InterWidget's customers were small companies. And only 5 per cent had more than 500 employees.

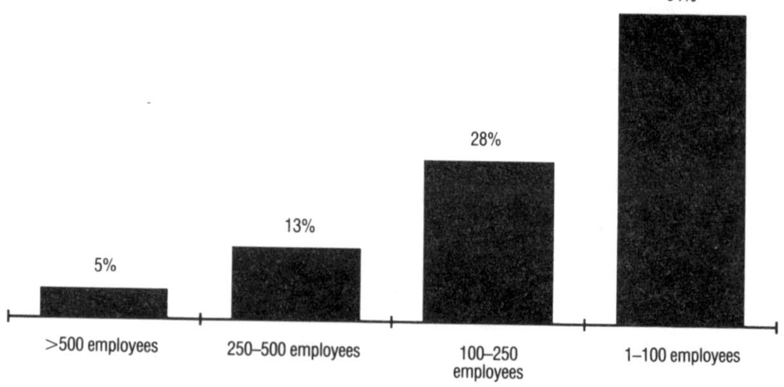

Figure 17 *The InterWidget customer base: all customers*

Looking deeper, Bill de Vries confirmed his own intuition that his best customers (Toppers) tended to be the larger machine tool manufacturers. But surprisingly, there were a number of very small companies among the Toppers – and some large companies who were Low Boys and clearly prospects for upgrading!

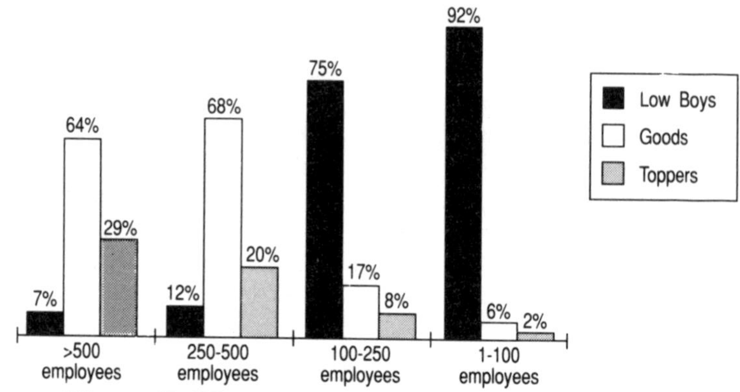

Figure 18 *The InterWidget customer base per customer type*

Bill then looked at his customer base against the entire market of machine tool manufacturers in his area. As Figure 19 reflects, the InterWidget customer base had proportionally twice as many larger companies than the market:

- 5 per cent of InterWidget customers had 500 employees versus 2 per cent for the market.
- 13 per cent of InterWidget customers had 250–500 employees as against 6 per cent for the market.

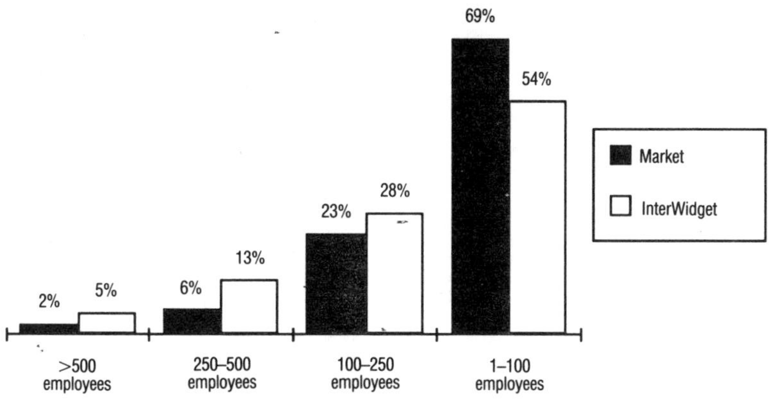

Figure 19 *InterWidget versus the market*

Continuing his market analysis, Bill took a look at his non-customers – the InterWidget prospects and suspects.

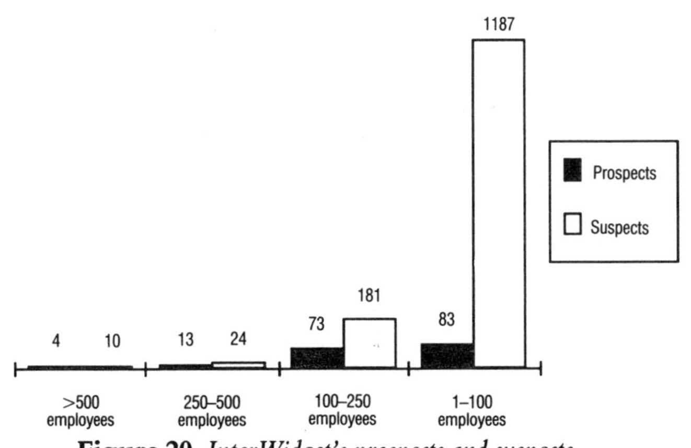

Figure 20 *InterWidget's prospects and suspects*

From this information, Bill calculated InterWidget's customer share – the percentage of companies of each machine tool manufacturer in the marketplace he could count as his customers. He found that he had an overall 34 per cent customer share. But among the larger companies, his customer share was 75 per cent.

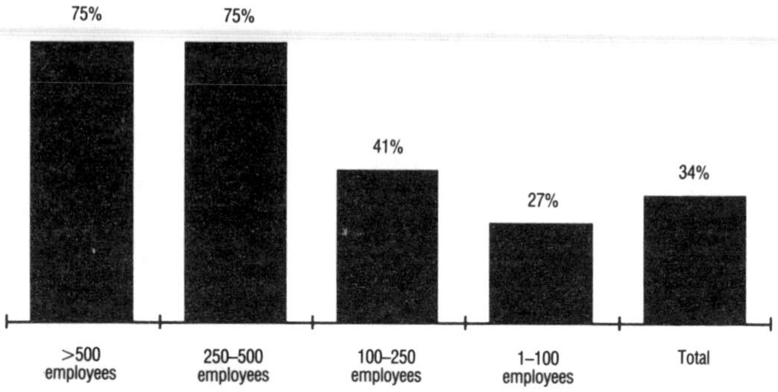

Figure 21 *The InterWidget customer share*

Bill de Vries knew that he wanted more Toppers. But he was already doing business with the great majority of larger companies in his area. Thus he concluded that the most likely source of the additional Topper customers he wanted were *already present in his existing customer base*!

And he vowed to move these customers up into the top of his customer pyramid by following the customer marketing strategy.

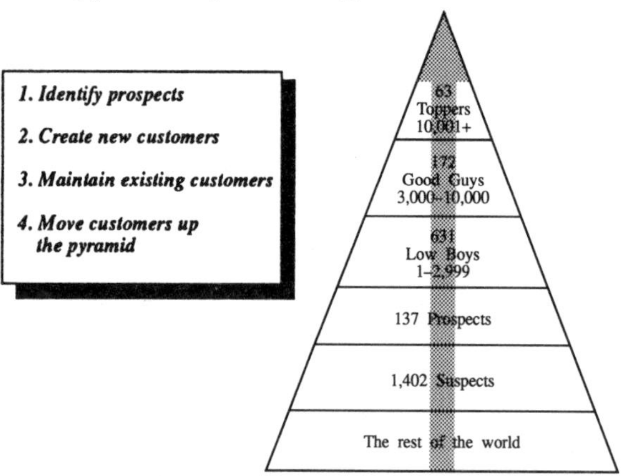

Figure 22 *The InterWidget strategy*

The next step was to set specific goals for identifying, creating, maintaining and upgrading InterWidget customers.

Step 4

Set Customer Goals

Customer goal setting is the most critical – and often the most difficult – step in customer marketing.

It is possible to set customer goals through rough guesstimates. And, indeed, you will have to make some decisions based on intuition, sales force estimates – with a bit of wishful thinking thrown in for good measure.

But since you will be setting specific goals, and measuring results, you should try to base your customer goals on a combination of statistical probabilities plus human input. And this we call *customer marketing ratings*.

Customer marketing ratings

The customer marketing rating is a numeric score for each customer, prospect and suspect to indicate where that company or individual 'belongs' in your customer pyramid. It is a combination of a *statistical score*, based on pure analysis of data, and a *contact score*, based on input provided by someone with knowledge of the customer, prospect or suspect.

As an example, let's take a law firm (yes, law firms have also put customer marketing concepts to good use!), which had created a customer pyramid with High, Medium and Low customers based on turnover. Using a scale from 1 to 10, the law firm assigned customer marketing ratings to these *prospect* categories:

Potential to be a High customer	18 or 19
Potential to be a Medium customer	15 to 17
Potential to be a Low customer	10 to 14

and to these *customer* categories:

Potential to be a High customer	28 or 29
Potential to be a Medium customer	25 to 27
Potential to be a Low customer	20 to 24

Statistical scores

As mentioned earlier, the common characteristics of your various customer types provide the basis for setting customer goals. When you are dealing with many characteristics and variables, you can get into the higher mathematical ground of regression analysis.

But often you can keep it simple. The law firm analysed its clients by industry sector and discovered, among other things, that large banks made up a high percentage of its top customers, and small retail stores formed the basis of its low-end customers.

Accordingly, *bank prospects* were assigned a statistical score, depending on their assets, from 18 or 19 and *bank customers* statistical scores of 28 or 29. Small retail stores, depending on their turnover, were allocated statistical scores of 10 to 14 for *prospects* and statistical scores of 20 to 24 for *customers*.

During the yearly exercise of developing, the law firm assigned to prospect Bank B a statistical score of 18. A retail customer, Retailer R, was given a statistical score of 22.

Contact scores

But a statistical score should be supplemented whenever possible with direct, up-to-date information based on the 'real world', such as the assessment of a salesperson or someone who has direct contact with or knowledge of the customer, prospect or suspect. And this knowledge can be converted into a *contact score*.

Obviously, contact scores cannot be used in the case of suspects with which there has been no contact or of whom there is no knowledge. In these instances your customer marketing rating will be solely on the statistical score – unless you decide to contact key suspects to provide information for a contact score, and thus turn them into prospects!

A contact score may be given a heavier weighting than the statistical score because the 'real world' input by the salespeople may be more accurate. But the statistical score provides a useful check against the subjective assessments of the sales force who, being human, sometimes allocate low contact scores to cover their own shortcomings.

In fact, if you have no statistical score you can still assign customer marketing ratings purely on contact scores with some success.

Let's see how the contact scores were applied in the law firm example.

A lawyer familiar with Bank B knew that the brother-in-law of Bank B's president was a senior partner in a competing law firm. Thus he gave Bank B a contact score of 11, because he judged that the law firm was only likely to get small assignments – if ever.

And another lawyer gave Retailer R a contact score of 28. Why? Because he knew that the retailer had just inherited millions, and was planning to undertake an expansion programme involving the take-over of a large number of shops, thereby generating a lot of legal fees!

By averaging the statistical scores and contact scores, the law firm arrived at these customer marketing ratings:

Customer marketing rating for Bank B = 14.5
(Average of statistical score of 18 and contact score of 11)

Customer marketing rating for Retailer R = 15
(Average of statistical score of 12 and contact score of 18)

Once you know from customer marketing ratings where customer, prospect and suspect 'belong' in your pyramid, you can estimate your chances of getting them there based on past experiences and the marketing and sales resources you will allocate to the effort.

Then you are in a position to answer these critical questions:

1. *Identification goals.* How many suspects in our pool can we convert to a prospect in the planning period?
2. *Creation goals.* Which suspects and prospects can we turn into what types of customer in the planning period?
3. *Maintenance goals.* Which customers can we maintain at current purchasing levels in the planning period?
4. *Upgrading goals.* Which customers can we move up the pyramid to a higher status in the planning period?

You then simply add or subtract the number of prospects and customers in your customer pyramid based on the answers to the above questions. Hey presto! You've got your customer goals!

Alternatively, you can match your customer goals to your business goals. If you want 10 per cent more turnover – or 20 per cent more margin – what kind of customer portfolio do you need to reach those goals?

Tip. It's not a bad idea to be a bit conservative at first – and don't forget to discount the number of customers who might drop down in spending, or disappear from view.

Setting customer goals – the InterWidget case

Bill de Vries decided to base his customer marketing ratings on the key factor which appeared to determine the potential of customers and prospects: the size of the customer in terms of personnel. To this information would be added the assessment of his sales representatives.

InterWidget statistical scores

To keep things simple, Bill simply matched statistical scores for *prospects*' with the number of employees, and allocated scores for the prospects' potential based on his analysis of the InterWidget customers. The statistical score for prospects ranged from 1 to 900. A prospect from 1 to 399 employees was judged to be a Low Boy candidate; from 400 to 599 a Good Guy candidate; and above 600 a Topper candidate.

InterWidget statistical score: prospects and suspects

Number of employees	*Statistical score*	*Type of customer candidate*
900 or more	900	Topper
800–899	800–899	
700–799	700–799	
600–699	600–699	
500–599	500–599	Good Guy
400–499	400–499	
300–399	300–399	Low Boy
200–299	200–299	
100–199	100–199	
1– 99	1– 99	

Statistical scores for *customers* were based on the same basic structure, but started with a lowest score of 1,001 and a highest score of 1,900.

InterWidget statistical score: customers

Number of employees	*Statistical score*	*Type of customer candidate*
900 or more	1,900	
800–899	1,800–1,899	
700–799	1,700–1,799	Topper
600–699	1,600–1,699	
500–599	1,500–1,599	Good Guy
400–499	1,400–1,499	
300–399	1,300–1,399	
200–299	1,200–1,299	Low Boy
100–199	1,100–1,199	
1– 99	1,001–1,099	

InterWidget contact scores

Bill kept the same point system for the InterWidget contact scores. But he decided to weight the contact scores by a factor of 2 since he felt that his sales force was well equipped to evaluate the real potential of a prospect or customer.

InterWidget contact score: prospects and suspects

Contact score (weighting 2×)	*Type of customer candidate*
Between 600 and 900	Topper
Between 400 and 599	Good Guy
Between 1 and 399	Low Boy

InterWidget contact score: customers

Contact score (weighting 2×)	*Type of customer potential*
Between 1,600 and 1,900	Topper
Between 1,400 and 1,599	Good Guy
Between 1,001 and 1,399	Low Boy

InterWidget customer marketing ratings
As the following indicate, InterWidget's customer marketing ratings were arrived at by adding the statistical score plus 2 times the contact score and dividing by 3.

InterWidget customer marketing rating: prospects and suspects

CM rating (SS+CS+CS)/3	*Type of customer candidate*
Between 600 and 900	Topper
Between 400 and 599	Good Guy
Between 1 and 399	Low Boy

InterWidget customer marketing rating: customers

CM rating (SS+CS+CS)/3	*Type of customer candidate*
Between 1,600 and 1,900	Topper
Between 1,400 and 1,599	Good Guy
Between 1,001 and 1,399	Low Boy

To implement the rating system, Bill had rating cards made up for each customer and prospect on which he put:

- The name of the prospect or customer.
- The date when scores were to be completed.
- The number of employees.
- The current place of the prospect or customer in the InterWidget customer pyramid.
- The statistical score, based on number of employees.

These cards were handed out to the sales force after a briefing on the system, with instructions for them to:

- Add a contact score.
- Calculate the customer marketing rating.
- Indicate the potential position in the pyramid.
- Write down the customer goal required to get the prospect or customer in that position.
- Estimate the chance of reaching that goal.

The cards looked like this:

InterWidget customer marketing rating card for prospects and suspects

Ajax Machine Tools Inc
No. of employees: 325

Current status:	Hot Prospect
Statistical score:	325
Contact score:	450
CM rating:	408
CM goal:	Create
Type:	Good Guy
Chance:	50%

InterWidget customer marketing rating card for customers

Eurotool Ltd
No. of employees: 435

Current status:	Low Boy
Statistical score:	1,435
Contact score:	1,850
CM rating:	1,712
CM goal:	Upgrade
Type:	Topper
Chance:	75%

Bill discovered that getting his salespeople involved in assigning customer marketing ratings for prospects and customers turned out to be highly motivating, and led to a better understanding of – and commitment to – customer marketing as the InterWidget way of doing business.

On the basis of these customer marketing ratings – and taking into consideration that they might lose 115 customers in the coming year owing to closures, mergers, bankruptcies, etc – Bill de Vries set these customer goals for InterWidget:

- Identification goals
  – identify 140 new prospects from the pool of suspects.
- Creation goals
  – 70 Low Boy customers
  – 15 Good Guy customers
  – 5 Topper customers
- Maintenance goals
  – 564 Low Boys
  – 172 Good Guys
  – 63 Toppers
- Upgrading goals
  – 67 Low Boys (42 to Good Guy status; 25 to Topper status)
  – 35 Good Guy to Topper status.

To make sure that everyone at InterWidget was aware of the company's customer goals, he compiled and distributed this pyramid chart to all staff:

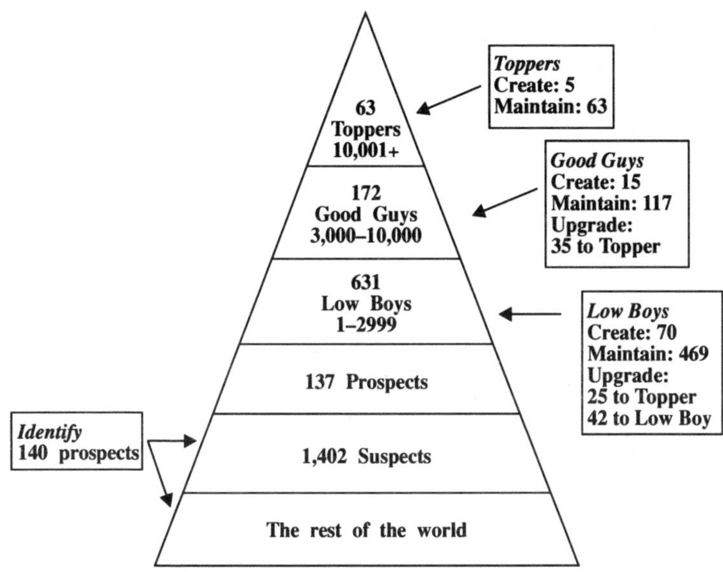

Figure 23 *InterWidget's customer goals*

Step 5

Develop a Customer Benefits Package

Once your customer goals are set, you must start thinking about developing a customer benefits package to help you reach them.

A customer benefits package is a cluster of services and rewards – in addition to your normal products and services – which you will offer to new and existing customers to help you meet your customer goals.

Take your time over this important step. Your customer benefits package may be the only factor which distinguishes you from your competitors. As such, it could be the primary reason why people will become your customers – and remain so.

The goodies in the customer benefits package need not be expensive. But the benefits must have a perceived rational or emotional value for the prospect when you promise them – and the benefits must provide satisfaction when you deliver them.

Benefits to identify potential customers

These benefits must be designed to get prospective customers to identify themselves to you as people or companies interested in your products and services.

For instance, if you are selling fancy CD players, you might want to develop a booklet 'Checklist for Selecting Your Next CD'. You can then offer this benefit free via an advertisement in a special interest magazine, *CD News*. Anyone ordering the booklet is most likely to be interested in your products – and he supplies you with his name, address and telephone number on the coupon.

Examples of commonly used benefits which encourage prospects to identify themselves to you include:

- Free (or almost free) booklet
- Free (or almost free) seminar
- Free (or almost free) sample

- Sweepstakes and games requiring a response
- Free (or almost free) gifts and premiums requiring a trial purchase.

Benefits to create new customers

You often have to offer a major benefit to stimulate people to start doing business with you on a regular basis and become your customer.

Book clubs, for instance, offer three books for only £6. But the new customer makes a commitment to buy four additional books within a year – and more than 90 per cent keep this promise.

Discount benefits

Many companies offer a 'starter' or 'get acquainted' discount to find new customers. The main advantage of a discount benefit is that it takes no time or energy to develop. The disadvantage is that discounts can dilute the perceived quality of your products or weaken your pricing structure.

I prefer to offer a free accessory, premium or service with perceived value, rather than giving a discount on the main product. Credit cards, for instance, waive the £50 entry fee but give no discount on the yearly membership fee. And machinery suppliers can offer the first six months of a service contract free.

'Member-get-member' and reference benefits

Your satisfied customers should be your best source of new customers. There is simply no stronger form of promotion than a recommendation from a satisfied customer. If you have satisfied customers, you will get new business from their recommendations. But why not stimulate and structure that process?

The shop which sold me a waterbed sent me an offer of a chance to win a free weekend away if I introduced a new prospect. They provided me with a special 'courtesy card' to give to family or friends to introduce them to the shop.

You can try the same thing, but also consider giving the same premium to both the existing and the new prospect.

In the business-to-business area, a classical 'member-get-member' activity may seem out of place. But there is nothing wrong in asking current customers for referrals for new business – and rewarding these referrals with an appropriate gesture, such as a special Christmas gift at the end of the year or a certificate for a dinner at a fancy restaurant for the customer and his partner.

Benefits to maintain customers

Customer marketing recognises this fact of business life:

> *Almost every business owes its existence to a regular flow of orders from regular customers. But many – if not most – marketing and sales managers devote the majority of their time – and budgets – to trying to get new customers!*

The result: regular customers become neglected. Or are left to cope with the not-always-customer-friendly departments in the company: accounts, production, technical service, etc.

Take the credit card business, for instance. You receive a personal letter signed by the managing director in the post designed to enlist you as a customer.

But once you become a customer, the personal letter from the managing director is replaced by monthly statements which sometimes contain threats about your late payment spewed by an anonymous 'Big Brother' computer, all in hard-to-read capital letters.

If you are treated this way, you may well be willing to respond to an offer from a competitive credit card company, hoping that they will treat you better as a regular customer.

Regular benefits and recognition for steady customers

So think hard about what benefits you want to offer your regular customers. They need not be expensive rewards, but rather gestures which recognise your appreciation for their business.

In all fairness, I must tell you about Diners Club which sent me a card on my birthday and a reward of 500 bonus points on their incentive scheme. (The next year, they coupled the birthday card with a wine offer – paid for, no doubt, by the vineyard!)

Why not send a 'birthday card' to your customers on the anniversary date of their first purchase or order?

Here are some other regular benefits you can offer steady customers – to keep them steady:

- Publications and 'magalogues'.

- Credit facilities or a credit card.
- Free Hotline service to handle problems.
- A Christmas gift in July (they will remember it!).

Immediate recognition for new customers

Once a new customer signs on, smother him/her/them with attention. In business markets, introduce the new customer to the company president or other high official. In consumer markets, a 'welcome aboard' letter signed by a director can serve the same function.

Other welcome aboard activities may include the offering of a credit facility or credit card or some benefit selected from the customer benefits package.

Special benefits for special customers

When you have a good customer, reward them royally and give them special treatment. It doesn't have to cost much to have a high impact.

As a 'frequent flyer', I am upgraded by TWA from tourist class to business class automatically – provided there is an empty seat. The marginal extra cost is more than made up by my frequent flying on TWA.

Compare this with my treatment as a member of KLM's Flying Dutchman Club: I was turned away from the business class lounge at JFK airport when travelling tourist class with my family. No benefit, no fly . . .

'The Advisory Board' benefit can also be offered to special customers with excellent results. This idea was developed years ago by *Chemical Week* magazine. Each year the publisher wrote to thousands of long-term subscribers asking them to serve on the *Chemical Week* Advisory Board. An impressive certificate, suitable for framing, was provided to those who agreed (the majority). A large percentage of the Advisory Board members cooperated with readership surveys, provided suggestions on an *ad hoc* basis to the Advisory Board Secretariat – and remained subscribers for the rest of their careers!

Benefits to get back 'lost' customers

Here is a key principle of customer marketing: never let a good customer get away from you – or stay away.

When you notice that a customer has left you, or is dropping away, take action. Ask if there is a problem. If so, fix the problem if at all possible. If you can't fix the problem, explain why and offer some kind of compensation.

The cost of getting a good customer back is generally only a fraction of the cost of creating a good customer.

And a dissatisfied ex-customer can do you damage that you'll never even know about! So phone them, send them a letter, pay a visit – do anything to prevent a good customer from slipping away.

Innovative retailer Murray Raphel sends his inactive customers a cheque or coupon worth $10. The reactivated customers usually spend many times the value of the credit. More important, they come back in the store, and tend to keep coming back.

Benefits to upgrade customers

It's nice to have steady customers. But it's even nicer to have steady customers who buy more!

Thus you must offer benefits to move your customers up the customer pyramid. It simply won't happen unless you stimulate the process with techniques such as:

- offering special terms if the customer extends his contract for a longer term;
- stimulating purchases with 'free gifts', premiums, discounts;
- stimulating additional purchases of an item on special terms;
- cross-selling: offering an item or service which complements something the customer already purchased;
- and anything else you can think of to stimulate more purchases and satisfaction.

You may also want to consider financial rewards: frequent buyer discounts, volume discounts, saving stamp plans and other techniques are often used to upgrade good customers and reward their loyalty.

Customer benefits package – the InterWidget case

Bill de Vries sat down with his marketing and sales staff and developed a number of benefits for InterWidget customers, prospects and suspects.

InterWidget benefits to identify customers

InterWidget had two customer identification programmes. For Suspects, it offered a *free booklet* on 'How to Improve Machine Tool Manufacturing', written by a recognised guru on the subject. This concept was expanded with free, half-day *seminars* on the same subject with the guru as the featured speaker.

People who requested the booklet or attended the seminar were screened, qualified and rated as to their status as prospects.

InterWidget benefits to create customers

Once it knew its prospects, InterWidget offered a variety of benefits to induce them to become customers. But these benefits were tailored to the type of customer to be created:

- A *one-year free service offer* was made to Topper customer candidates.
- A *three-month free trial* of InterWidget products was offered to Good Guy candidates.
- A *free demonstration* and presentation of Widget products was offered to Low Boy candidates.

InterWidget benefits to maintain customers

- InterWidget extended its highly successful customer satisfaction survey as an ongoing customer satisfaction programme consisting of follow-up calls to customers within one week after a shipment was delivered or service repair was made. The customers were asked if their shipment had arrived and was as ordered. The service customers were asked if the problem was resolved. If there was any dissatisfaction, immediate action was taken and the customer was notified. In all cases, the customers received a relevant 'personal' letter from Bill de Vries.
- A Widget Users Group (WUG) was also established for all customers. WUG had quarterly meetings combining seminars plus social entertainment and an informative newsletter. The WUG kept InterWidget in touch with its customers, and provided a forum for exchanging ideas.
- Topper customers were invited to join 'The Inner Circle' of WUG which featured a yearly 'study trip' to visit machine tool manufacturers in exotic, far-off places. These proved to be very popular. And while the cost was high, so was the payoff!

InterWidget benefits to upgrade customers

- To upgrade Good customers to Topper status, InterWidget held out the promise of joining 'The Inner Circle' – the yearly study trip.
- Low Boy customers were enticed to move up to Good status as the yearly service contract fee was waived on some products.

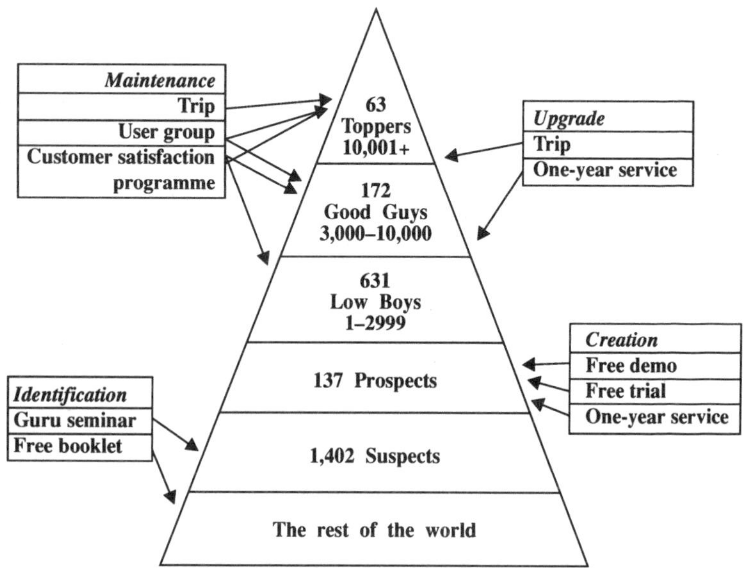

Figure 24 *InterWidget customer benefits*

Step 6

Select Methods and Media

As discussed in Part 1 of this book, virtually every marketing and sales medium and method can be used for customer marketing. The trick is to select methods and media which will:

- succeed in reaching the goal of identifying, creating, maintaining and upgrading customers;
- do the job for the least cost.

There are no hard and fast rules about which medium to apply when and where. But it is obvious that the most personal, most effective – and most expensive – media and methods may be required to achieve the toughest assignments: *creating* and *upgrading* customers.

Which media and methods are best for you? You may wish to analyse your own situation by reviewing the descriptions of the

Personal media	*Identify*	*Create*	*Maintain*	*Upgrade*
• External sales force	☐	☐	☐	☐
• Internal sales force	☐	☐	☐	☐
• Support/Service staff	☐	☐	☐	☐
• Business mail and calls	☐	☐	☐	☐
• Business events (shows, seminars)	☐	☐	☐	☐
Semi-personal media				
• Telemarketing	☐	☐	☐	☐
• Direct mail	☐	☐	☐	☐
Non-personal media				
• Response advertising	☐	☐	☐	☐
• Radio and TV commercials	☐	☐	☐	☐
• Publicity	☐	☐	☐	☐
• Yellow Pages	☐	☐	☐	☐
• POS, coupons, etc	☐	☐	☐	☐

Figure 25 *Methods and media checklist*

key customer marketing media and methods below. Then tick off which you are using – or should be using – to identify, acquire, maintain and upgrade your customers.

Personal media and methods

- *External sales force*
  No medium is so effective in making, keeping and upgrading customers as a salesperson who is able to listen to the prospect, identify his problem and translate the salesperson's product into a solution. But there is also no more expensive medium: the cost per sales call is over £75 in many countries – and rising.
- *Internal sales force*
  Less expensive, of course, than the external sales force, and normally very cost-effective when handling existing customers. Less useful for converting prospects to first-time buyers unless the product or service has a low price or other barrier.
- *Support/Service staff*
  Many companies are discovering that their support, service and maintenance people can become a secret weapon in the competitive battle for customers and sales. Why? Because these people are often able to enter a customer's premises, talk with the users and decision makers in a non-threatening, non-sales situation, and find out what the customer's needs and problems are. The customer may be hesitant to discuss his equipment problems with the salesman with an order form in his blue suit. But the bespectacled service fellow in jeans is no threat. Success in using support and service staff as marketing media comes when you train them to spot business opportunities, give them the tools (such as structured visit report forms) and, above all, give them the incentives (both monetary and praise) for a job well done.
- *Business mail*
  Business mail is a sales visit substitute. Instead of visiting the customer or prospect, the salesperson writes a 'personal' note. For example, the people who rent out copying machines produce from their customer database 'personal letters' for their salespeople to sign which read something like this:

> Dear Joe
>
> Just a short note to let you know that I heard around the office that the monthly rental price of the WIDGETS may go up by 5 per cent next year. Now, I think that I can get my boss to keep the price for you the same as this year if you can commit now. Just put your signature on the enclosed extension request, and I'll take care of everything. Please phone if you have any questions.
>
> Best regards,
>
> Sam Salesperson

And after signing the computer-produced letter, the salesperson then writes a personal note in his or her own handwriting:

> PS Give my regards to Mary.

Such 'personal' letters are sent out by the hundreds – or thousands, in some cases.

- *Business phone calls*
  Business phone calls work like business mail, but instead of a letter use a semi-programmed telephone script which the salesperson can adapt for each customer he or she phones.
- *Business events (shows, exhibitions, seminars, etc)*
  Business events are useful for identifying potential customers and for maintaining the relationship with current customers. They can be cost-effective since salesperson time can be leveraged in a 'one-on-many' group situation instead of the normal 'one-to-one' sales situation.

Semi-personal media

- *Telemarketing*
  Telemarketing is the fastest growing customer marketing medium. Although cost per contact is higher than for direct mail, it is not unusual to make effective contact with 50 to 80 per cent or more designated persons in a market segment. Telemarketing can also be powerful and persuasive, if handled properly. (If poorly done, telemarketing can kill

your reputation!) Telemarketing is also quite flexible. After only 50 to 100 calls, you know whether or not your list, offer and script need adjustment.

- *Direct mail*
  Direct mail has many advantages for customer marketing. It is highly targeted: you can send it to very specific groups and segments. It is also reasonably personal since it is addressed to one individual, and 'signed' by another. And most people perceive a letter as the most personal form of written communication between human beings. Primary disadvantages: mailing costs are rising and sure to go higher – but response rates remain the same or are falling. Direct mail is also a bit inflexible: there is a lead time of a month or two to get a major mailing sent, and you don't know your success until a week or a month after the mailing date.

Non-personal media

- *Response advertising*
  This can be highly cost-effective for identifying prospects and even generating sales for lower-priced articles. Cost per contact is generally low, normally below 5p per subscriber.
- *Radio and TV commercials*
  Response from radio commercials may work – but usually not as effectively as TV commercials, where a product/service can be demonstrated and the response address and/or telephone number can be shown. Response TV is becoming more popular with the development of highly segmented cable services: the cost goes down while the chance of reaching a particular segment goes up.
- *Publicity*
  Publicity and free press play can be a highly effective and cheap customer marketing medium. (Just make sure you get your address or telephone number in the article!)
- *Yellow Pages*
  Sometimes excellent for having potential customers identify themselves to you. (By mistake, my company name is listed – in very small type face like this – in the Yellow Pages under 'Home computers'. And yet I get at least one call a week asking for Commodore 64 software!)

- *Point-of-sale, coupons, on-pack/in-pack folders, etc*
  In fact, just about any medium – including bookmatches – can be used for customer marketing. As long as it has a realistic chance of contributing to the customer marketing objectives of identifying, creating, keeping and developing customers.

Methods and media – the InterWidget case

Bill de Vries found that while talking about the benefits package with his marketing and sales staff, the discussion quickly turned to how these benefits would be communicated. And so they stayed an extra hour and came up with these choices of methods and media.

InterWidget methods and media to identify customers

- *Response advertisements* in trade publications offering the free booklet were targeted at suspects.
- *Direct mail* offering the guru seminar was sent to prospect and suspect decision makers.
- *Telemarketing* was used to qualify leads and follow up non-response.

InterWidget methods and media to create customers

- The *external sales force* was the only logical way for InterWidget to acquire new business.

InterWidget methods and media to maintain customers

- Regular sales and service contacts via the *internal sales force* were the primary customer maintenance media, supplemented by:
- *Courtesy visits* by the external sales force to Topper customers; and
- *Business calls* and *business mail* to both Topper and Good customers.

InterWidget methods and media to upgrade customers

- The *external sales force* was focused on upgrading Good customers.

- The *internal sales force* had the task of upgrading Low Boy customers.

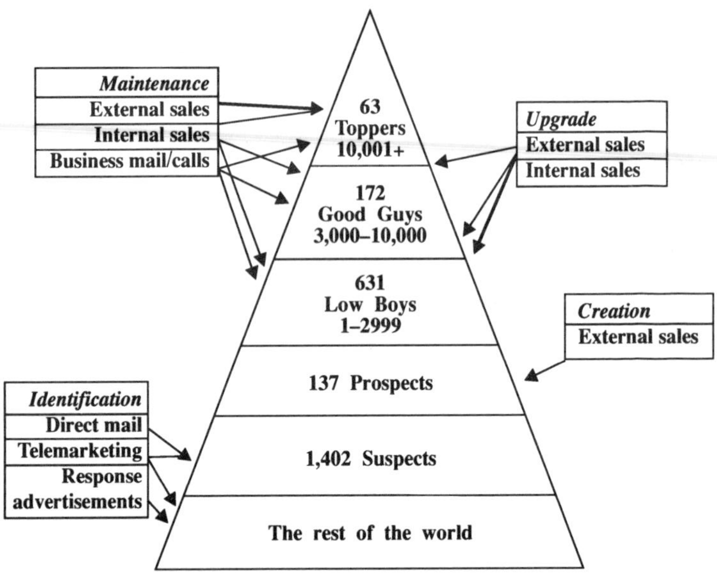

Figure 26 *InterWidget methods and media*

Customer marketing budget

Bill de Vries and his staff made detailed budgets and plans for implementing the customer benefits package and the selling methods and media. A summary of their efforts is illustrated. (Details can be found in the InterWidget spreadsheets.)

Notice that the InterWidget customer marketing budget allocates funds three ways:

- by customer goals (identification, creation, maintenance and upgrading);
- per type of method/media (customer benefits, sales force and semi/non-personal);
- per customer (suspects/prospects, Low Boys, Goods and Toppers).

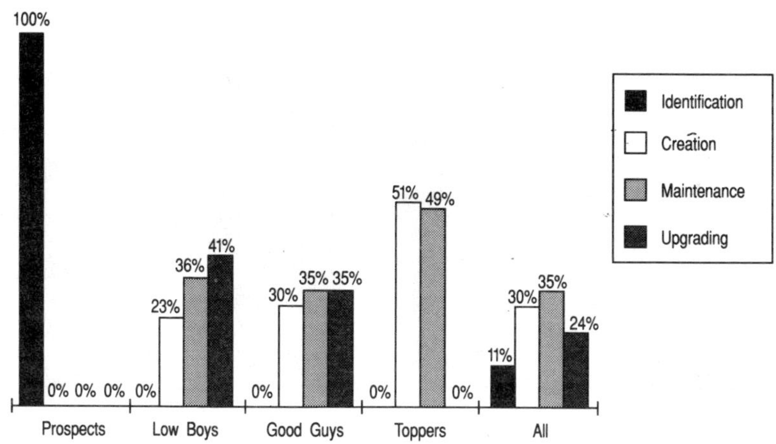

Figure 27 *Customer marketing budget: per customer goal*

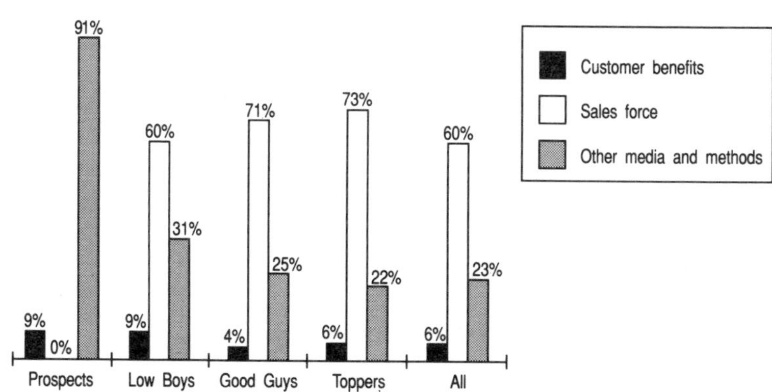

Figure 28 *Customer marketing budget: per methods and media*

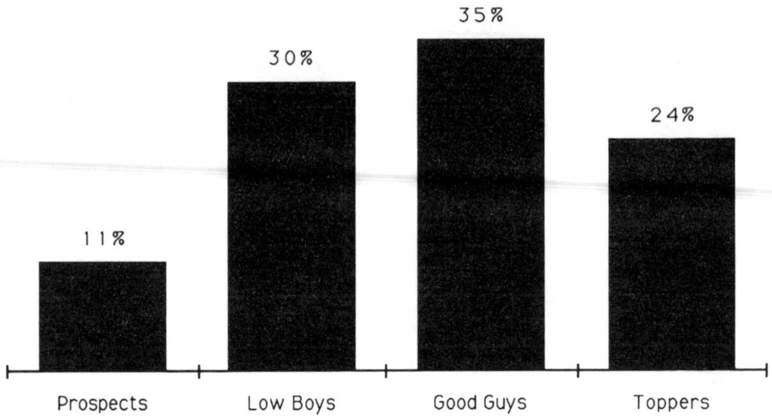

Figure 29 *Customer marketing budget: per customer type*

Step 7

Get Customer Orientated

Customer marketing simply won't work unless you and everyone else in your company have a strong customer orientation. What is a customer orientation?

Well, you have it when you know who your customers are . . . you know what they want and expect from you . . . you know what they think about you . . . you are always seeking more customers . . . you are determined never to lose a customer . . . you realise that, without customers, you might as well shut the door and go home.

A customer orientation doesn't evolve automatically. It must be actively introduced into an organisation, nurtured and maintained until it becomes an integral part of the company culture. Even then, constant monitoring is necessary to ensure that customer orientation sticks.

Customer orientation – the InterWidget case

Here are the programmes and activities which Bill de Vries used to introduce a customer orientation at InterWidget:

Phone a customer a day programme
Bill has an arrangement with his secretary to phone one customer a day. And when he gets the customer on the phone he says: 'Good morning, Mr Customer. I'm Bill de Vries of InterWidget, and I'm phoning for two reasons. First, I want you to know how much we appreciate your business. We're really proud to count you among our customers.'

Bill can almost hear the customer think: 'What's going on here? This is the first time anybody from InterWidget has phoned without trying to sell me something! What's going to happen next?' Bill then continues with: 'The second point, Mr Customer, is that I'd like your advice, ideas and opinions on how we can do a better job for you.'

And the customer thinks: 'Gosh, these people from InterWidget are OK. Because they are asking the smartest man in the world for advice – me!'

More often than not, Bill then hears things like: 'Did you know that it sometimes takes more than a minute before someone answers your phone.' Or 'I think your service department is excellent – they need a bit more recognition.' Or 'We'd like to do more business with you, but only if we get a credit account. Can we talk about it?' Or 'I've got no problem with InterWidget – in fact, now that you're on the phone, I'd like to discuss a new order.'

Key account contact by management

InterWidget's key accounts represented their profitable business. Bill makes sure that he and his other managers have personal contact with key accounts at least once a month.

Rewards for 'customer results'

Salespeople are generally rewarded for sales volume. Bill de Vries added rewards for customer results as well at InterWidget: X points for gaining a new customer, minus X points for losing a customer. Implementing customer scores – among the sales force and sales management – worked wonders for InterWidget.

Service staff incentives to develop customers

InterWidget's service and support staff have intensive customer contact. Thus they are in a position to identify customer needs and new business opportunities. So Bill offered them incentives, both tangible (bonus, trips, etc) and intangible (awards and recognition). But incentives were not enough. His service and support staff also needed training or other tools such as a 'Business Opportunities Report Form' to be filled in after each visit to a customer site.

Training for the 'front-line troops' . . .

At InterWidget, as at most companies, telephonists, receptionists, secretaries and the accounts staff have frequent customer contact. As such, they are the front-line troops of customer marketing. Thus the way they deal with customers and prospects determines to a large extent attitudes towards your organisation. Bill scheduled telephone skills training programmes for his front-line troops. But he also found it doesn't hurt to check out the troops once in a while. He phones his switchboard regularly to see how callers are handled, and reviews the methods his credit controllers use to 'encourage' customers to pay overdue invoices.

Customer orientation programmes for everybody

Last, but certainly not least, Bill de Vries made sure that every employee was aware of the company's customer goals – and how far along they all were in meeting them. He also announced the results of market research reports on how InterWidget's customers – and non-customers – rated the company and the competition.

Bill even had some video tapes made of some happy – and not so happy – customers. He had these shown to all staff – including the workers on the factory floor. For some of them, it was the first time they had ever laid eyes on an InterWidget customer! The improvement in higher quality was immediately measurable.

Step 8

Record Customer Behaviour

Customer marketing requires you to record customer behaviour such as:

- RFM indicators per customer
- products purchased
- media methods creating transactions
- returns
- payment history.

With this information you can learn how to fine-tune your customer marketing activities, to make more customers, more profits and incur lower costs.

But how can you record customer behaviour if you have thousands of customers? Some businesses which rely on computer-based order processing systems have no major problem, ie banks, credit card companies, mail order, publications, etc.

Retailers who want to use customer marketing usually have to introduce some kind of credit or customer card which brings together information about the customer and products purchased at the cash register.

Fast-moving consumer goods companies are experimenting with bonus stamp systems and 'club'-type activities.

It is not always easy to record customer data in the consumer marketplace. But the use of universal product codes plus data-capturing hardware such as optical readers and light pens are making the process easier.

Recording customer behaviour – the InterWidget case

InterWidget spent considerable time and effort keeping track of customer behaviour and registering that behaviour in their customer database. At the end of the year, Bill made up a new pyramid showing InterWidget's 'customer results'.

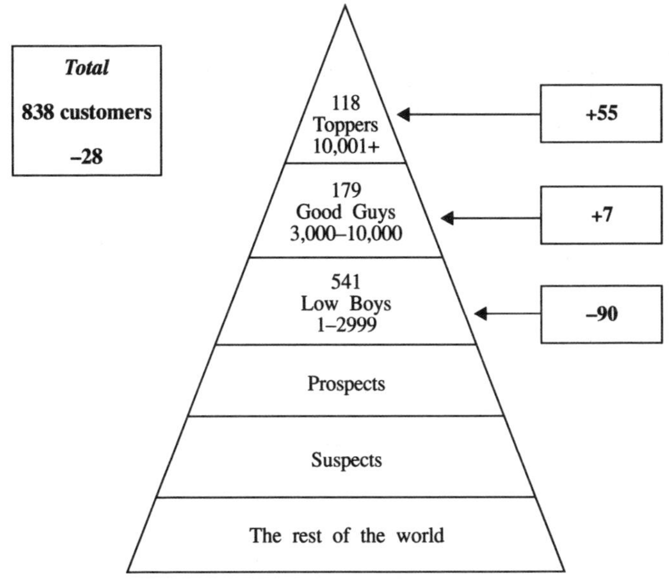

Figure 30 *InterWidget's customer pyramid after customer marketing*

And as Figure 31 shows, InterWidget's customer results pretty much matched the customer goals set at the beginning of the year.

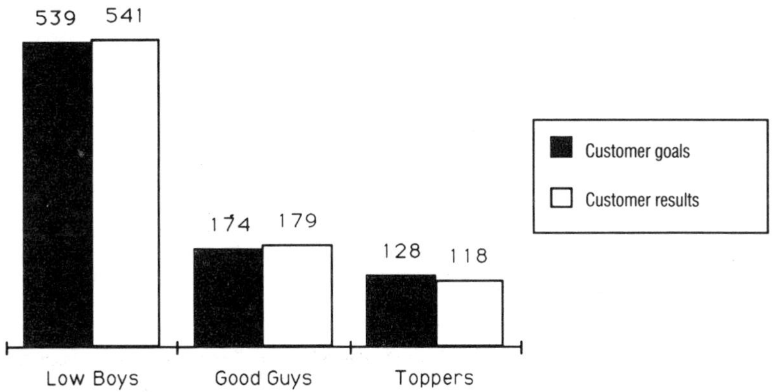

Figure 31 *Customer goals versus customer results*

Step 9

Analyse Results

Customer marketing is a learning process based on a continuing flow of customer and market information. And when this information is analysed, you learn some lessons. And then you apply the lessons learned to revisions in your marketing efforts.

The kinds of question you can answer from effective customer marketing include:

- Who are our clients?
- Who buys what?
- Which clients are profitable? Which are not?
- Who decides, buys and uses our products?
- Which distribution channel works best?
- Which customer benefits work best?
- Which media, methods and messages work best?
- What is the ROI on our marketing money?
- How should we allocate our marketing budget?

Analysing results – the InterWidget case

Bill de Vries was quite pleased about the bottom line impact of customer marketing on InterWidget's financial results: more than 100 per cent increase in profits despite:

- a 3 per cent increase in marketing and sales costs;
- a 10 per cent increase in overheads to set up and manage the customer database; and
- a 3 per cent decrease in the number of customers!

Here is how it looked on a chart:

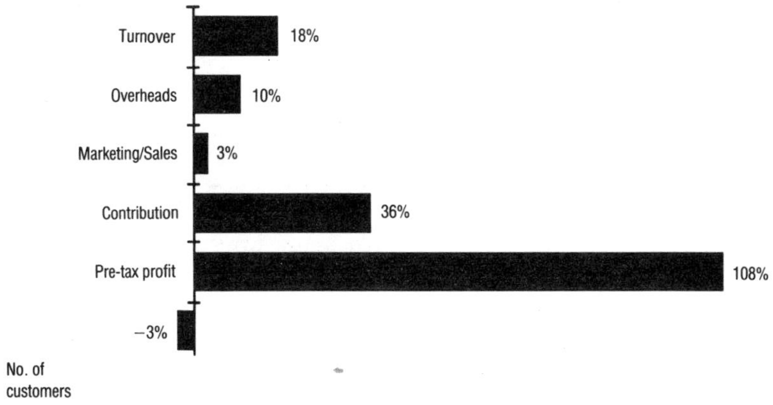

Figure 32 *Customer marketing: the profit pay-off for InterWidget*

But to really understand the impact of customer marketing on InterWidget, Bill went to the primary source of the good news – the InterWidget customers. He made this comparison of changes which occurred among each customer type:

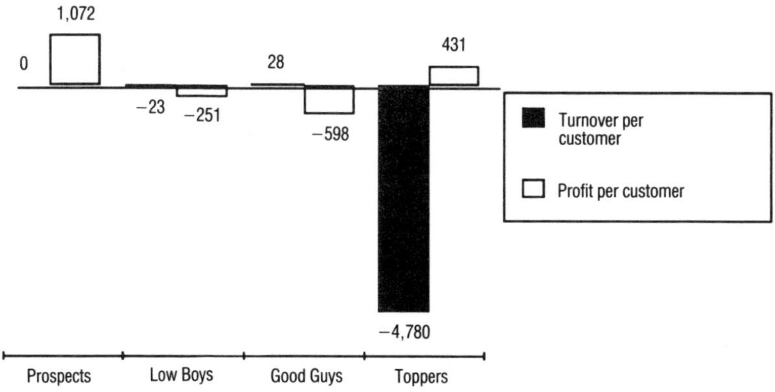

Figure 33 *Financial impact: per customer type*

Bill de Vries took a lot of time to look at the before/after analysis. He concluded that the real reasons for the customer marketing profit pay-off were to be seen in two categories: Prospects and Toppers.

- *Prospects*. Bill noticed that marketing and sales costs per prospect decreased substantially. This was a direct result of selecting the right methods and media, ie replacing sales force prospecting efforts with semi- and non-personal media and methods.
- *Toppers*. Turnover per customer dropped 4,780. This apparent decrease in spending reflected the fact that new acquisitions and upgrades from the Low Boy and Good Guy categories joined Topper status during the year, thus diluting Topper turnover per customer performance for the entire period.

  But profit per Topper customer increased substantially, again owing to a better allocation of marketing and sales budget and effort.

As a result, overall results per customer were an increase in turnover and profit per customer of £906 and £293 respectively.

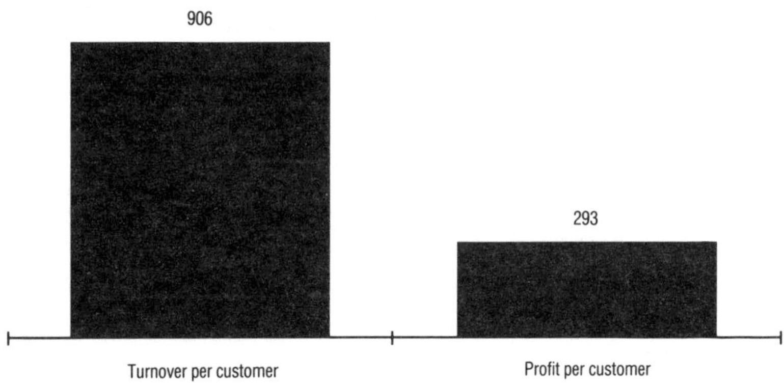

Figure 34 *Financial impact: all customers*

Bill's final conclusion was that InterWidget's profit pay-off from customer marketing would continue – or even increase – in the following year. He knew he could reduce sales and marketing costs even more because his primary task would be maintaining InterWidget's new Toppers, an activity which should cost less time and money than upgrading them.

And the newly upgraded and acquired customers, if maintained, would perform for the entire year, thus bringing up turnover and profits per customer category across the board.

Step 10

Revise Your Customer Programmes

When you have made your analysis, you should know what worked, what didn't and why. And in the future you can focus on what works:

- winning segments;
- winning products;
- winning benefits;
- winning media/methods.

The losers you dump without ceremony, and pledge to yourself never to make the same mistake twice.

But remember: today's winner is tomorrow's loser. The world around you, your competitors, the technology, your customers' needs and wants keep changing. So you have to keep on gathering customer marketing information, keep on analysing it, keep on testing.

Revising customer programmes – the InterWidget case

Bill de Vries was very satisfied with the results of customer marketing. The customer satisfaction programme was especially successful, identifying a lot of customer needs which had not been identified in the past. And since the response from customers led to personal discussions, a number of unexpected orders closed. It paid for itself.

But Bill and his staff also noted a number of activities and areas which could have been better. For instance:

- The Widget User Group took a lot of time and energy to organise – and sometimes the meetings turned into 'gripe sessions'. The activity will be streamlined.

- While the InterWidget marketing and sales managers got along personally, there was a good deal of confusion over who was responsible for which activity, especially telemarketing.
- The guru seminar was a disappointment. The man arrived late and delivered his speech in a routine manner. Fortunately, the audience was not very large. The programme was replaced by a one-day Widget Workshop using Widget technicians as trainers.
- Despite an investment of almost £60,000 in a customer database – and a person to manage it – the system was difficult for many salespeople to use, and it took too much time to get the information Bill wanted every month.

As Bill de Vries discovered, internal factors more often than not have a great impact on the success of your marketing and sales efforts. If some of the problems he encountered seem familiar, you may wish to subject your business to a customer marketing audit as explained in Part 3.

Customer Marketing Spreadsheets

The following pages contain the spreadsheets which Bill de Vries at InterWidget used to develop his customer marketing analyses and plans, and are referred to in the preceding pages. You may want to base your own spreadsheets on this model.

InterWidget financial results last year

Turnover	3,642,954
Cost of product	1,827,571
Gross margin	1,814,973
Marketing/Salespeople	601,950
Marketing/Sales: other	396,616
Total marketing/sales	998,566
Contribution	816,407
Overheads	596,297
Pre-tax profit	220,110
Number of customers	866
Turnover per customer	4,207
Pre-tax profit per customer	254

Financial analysis of InterWidget – last year's results

Financial analysis per customer type	*Prospects*	*Low Boy customers*	*Good customers*	*Topper customers*	*Total*
Number of prospects	137				137
Number of customers		631	172	63	866
Turnover	0	943,940	1,211,871	1,487,143	3,642,954
Total cost of product	0	486,487	605,638	735,446	1,827,571
Total/Gross margin	0	457,003	606,233	751,737	1,814,973
Marketing/Sales: salespeople	150,488	150,488	150,488	150,488	601,950
Marketing/Sales: other	99,154	99,154	99,154	99,154	396,616
Total marketing/sales	249,642	249,642	249,642	249,642	998,566
Contribution	– 249,642	207,361	356,592	502,096	816,407
Overheads	149,074	149,074	149,074	149,074	596,297
Pre-tax profit	– 398,716	58,287	207,517	353,021	220,110
Profit as % of sales	NA	6%	17%	24%	6%
Marketing/Sales ROI	– 160%	23%	83%	141%	22%
% customers	NA	73%	20%	7%	100%
% turnover	NA	26%	33%	41%	100%
% profit	NA	9%	34%	57%	100%
Financial analysis per customer type	*Prospects*	*Low Boy customers*	*Good customers*	*Topper customers*	*Total*
Turnover per customer	0	1,496	7,046	23,605	4,207
Margin per customer	0	724	3,525	11,932	2,096
Marketing and sales/costs per customer	1,822	396	1,451	3,963	1,153
Contribution per customer	– 1,822	329	1,206	5,660	580
Overheads per customer	1,088	236	867	2,366	689
Pre-tax profit per customer	– 2,910	92	1,206	5,604	254
Breakeven no. of customers	NA	551	113	33	761

InterWidget market analysis – customer base

Customer base description (actual)	*Low Boy customers*	*Good customers*	*Topper customers*	*Total*
>500 employees	3	27	12	42
250–500 employees	13	74	22	109
100–250 employees	183	42	19	244
1–100 employees	432	29	10	471
Total customers	631	172	63	866

Customer base description (%)	*Low Boy customers*	*Good customers*	*Topper customers*	*All customers*
>500 employees	7%	64%	29%	5%
250–500 employees	12%	68%	20%	13%
100–250 employees	75%	17%	8%	28%
1–100 employees	92%	6%	2%	54%
Total customers	73%	20%	7%	100%

InterWidget market analysis – Market description:
Machine tool industry

Market size (companies):

>500 employees	56	2%
250–500 employees	146	6%
100–250 employees	598	23%
1–100 employees	1,748	69%
Total market	2,548	100%

Non-customer distribution (actual)	*Prospect distribution*	*Suspect distribution*	*All non-customers*
>500 employees	4	10	14
250–500 employees	13	24	37
100–250 employees	73	281	354
1–100 employees	83	1,194	1,277
Total non-customers	173	1,509	1,682

Non-customer distribution (%)	*Prospect distribution*	*Suspect distribution*	*All non-customers*
>500 employees	2%	1%	1%
250–500 employees	8%	2%	2%
100–250 employees	42%	19%	21%
1–100 employees	48%	79%	76%
Total non-customers	10%	90%	100%

Customer share by type and total	*Low Boy customers*	*Good customers*	*Topper customers*	*Share per segment*
>500 employees	5%	48%	21%	75%
250–500 employees	9%	51%	15%	75%
100–250 employees	31%	7%	3%	41%
1–100 employees	25%	2%	1%	27%
Overall share	25%	7%	2%	34%

InterWidget customer goals

Customer goals next year	*Prospects*	*Low Boy customers*	*Good customers*	*Topper customers*	*Total*
Prospects (start)	137				137
Existing customers (start)		631	172	63	866
Expected fall-off	60	95	20	0	115
Existing customers (net)	NA	536	152	63	751
Identification goals	140				140
Creation goals	NA	70	15	5	90
Maintenance goals	NA	469	117	63	649
Upgrading goals					
Upgrade to Toppers	NA	25	35	0	60
Upgrade to Good	NA	42	0	0	42
Total upgrade out	NA	67	35	0	102
Total upgrade in	NA	0	42	60	102
Totals after plan period					
Prospects	217				217
Customers		539	174	128	841

Customer maintenance budget

Methods and media budget – maintenance	*Prospects*	*Low Boy customers*	*Good customers*	*Topper customers*	*Total*
Customer maintain goals	NA	469	117	63	649
Personal media					
• External sales force	0	20,000	40,000	80,000	140,000
• Internal sales force	0	20,000	30,000	10,000	60,000
Subtotal sales force	0	40,000	70,000	90,000	200,000
• Business mail/calls	0	5,000	3,000	2,000	10,000
• User group/trips/ seminar	0	5,000	3,000	5,000	13,000
Semi-personal media					
• Direct mail shots	0	0	0	0	0
• Newsletter	0	5,000	2,000	1,000	8,000
• Telemarketing/ outbound	0	0	0	0	0
• Customer service programme	0	50,000	40,000	20,000	110,000
Non-personal media					
• Coupon advertising	0	0	0	0	0
• Response radio/TV ads	0	0	0	0	0
• Publicity/PR	0	3,000	2,000	1,000	6,000
• Other	0	0	0	0	0
Subtotal other non-sales	0	68,000	50,000	29,000	147,000
Subtotal maintenance	0	108,000	120,000	119,000	347,000

Customer upgrading budget

Methods and media budget – upgrading	*Prospects*	*Low Boy customers*	*Good customers*	*Topper customers*	*Total*
Upgrade to Toppers	NA	25	35	0	60
Upgrade to Good	NA	42	0	0	42
Total upgrade out	NA	67	35	0	102
Total upgrade in	NA	0	42	60	102
Personal media					
• External sales force	0	80,000	95,000	0	175,000
• Internal sales force	0	25,000	20,000	0	45,000
Subtotal sales force	0	105,000	115,000	0	220,000
• Business mail/calls	0	2,000	1,000	0	3,000
• User group/trips/ seminar	0	5,000	3,000	0	8,000
Semi-personal media					
• Direct mail shots	0	2,000	0	0	2,000
• Newsletter	0	2,000	0	0	2,000
• Telemarketing/ outbound	0	7,000	1,000	0	8,000
• Customer service programme	0	0	0	0	0
Non-personal media					
• Coupon advertising	0	0	0	0	0
• Response radio/TV ads	0	0	0	0	0
• Publicity/PR	0	0	0	0	0
• Other	0	0	0	0	0
Subtotal other non-sales	0	18,000	5,000	0	23,000
Subtotal upgrading	0	123,000	120,000	0	243,000

Customer identification and creation budget

Methods and media budget – identify and create	*Prospects*	*Low Boy customers*	*Good customers*	*Topper customers*	*Total*
Prospecting goals	140				
Customer creation goals		70	15	5	90
Personal media					
• External sales force	0	10,000	25,000	50,000	85,000
• Internal sales force	0	25,000	35,000	35,000	95,000
Subtotal sales force	0	35,000	60,000	85,000	180,000
• Business mail/calls	0	0	0	0	0
• User group/trips/ seminar	10,000	0	5,000	7,000	22,000
Semi-personal media					
• Direct mail shots	35,000	15,000	15,000	10,000	75,000
• Newsletter	0	5,000	10,000	5,000	20,000
• Telemarketing/ outbound	18,000	10,000	10,000	10,000	48,000
• Customer service programme	0	0	0	0	0
Non-personal media					
• Coupon advertising	45,000	0	0	0	45,000
• Response radio/TV ads	0	0	0	0	0
• Publicity/PR	5,000	5,000	5,000	5,000	20,000
• Other	0	0	0	0	0
Subtotal other non-sales	113,000	35,000	45,000	37,000	230,000
Subtotal identification	113,000				113,000
Subtotal creation		70,000	105,000	122,000	297,000

Customer marketing budget per customer type

Methods and media budget – customer type	*Prospects*	*Low Boy customers*	*Good customers*	*Topper customers*	*Total*
Number	140	539	174	128	841
Personal media					
• External sales force	0	110,000	160,000	130,000	400,000
• Internal sales force	0	70,000	85,000	45,000	200,000
Subtotal sales force	0	180,000	245,000	175,000	600,000
• Business mail/calls	0	7,000	4,000	2,000	13,000
• User group/trips/ seminar	10,000	10,000	11,000	12,000	43,000
Semi-personal media					
• Direct mail shots	35,000	17,000	15,000	10,000	77,000
• Newsletter	0	12,000	12,000	6,000	30,000
• Telemarketing/ outbound	18,000	17,000	11,000	10,000	56,000
• Customer service programme	0	50,000	40,000	20,000	110,000
Non-personal media					
• Coupon advertising	45,000	0	0	0	45,000
• Response radio/TV ads	0	0	0	0	0
• Publicity/PR	5,000	8,000	7,000	6,000	26,000
• Other	0	0	0	0	0
Subtotal other	113,000	121,000	100,000	66,000	400,000
Grand total	113,000	301,000	345,000	241,000	1,000,000
% marketing budget	11%	30%	35%	24%	100%
Cost per type	807	558	1,983	1,883	1,189

Customer marketing budget per customer goal

Methods and media budget – customer goals	*Identify prospects*	*Create customers*	*Maintain customers*	*Upgrade customers*	*Total*
Prospect goals	140				
Customer goals		90	649	102	841
Personal media					
• External sales force	0	85,000	140,000	175,000	400,000
• Internal sales force	0	95,000	60,000	45,000	200,000
Subtotal sales force	0	180,000	200,000	220,000	600,000
• Business mail/calls	0	0	10,000	3,000	13,000
• User group/trips/ seminar	10,000	12,000	13,000	8,000	43,000
Semi-personal media					
• Direct mail shots	35,000	40,000	0	2,000	77,000
• Direct mail catalogues	0	20,000	8,000	2,000	30,000
• Telemarketing/ outbound	18,000	30,000	0	8,000	56,000
• Customer satisfaction	0	0	110,000	0	110,000
Non-personal media					
• Coupon advertising	45,000	0	0	0	45,000
• Response radio/TV ads	0	0	0	0	0
• Publicity/PR	5,000	15,000	6,000	0	26,000
• Other	0	0	0	0	0
Subtotal other	113,000	117,000	147,000	23,000	400,000
Grand total	113,000	297,000	347,000	243,000	1,000,000
% marketing budget	11%	30%	35%	24%	100%
Cost per prospect	807				807
Cost per customer		3,300	535	2,382	1,189

Customer marketing budget – summary

Methods and media budget – summary	*Suspects/ Prospects*	*Low Boy customers*	*Good customers*	*Topper customers*	*Total*	*% of budget*
Customer identification						
Customer benefits, etc	10,000	0	0	0	0	0%
External/Internal sales	0	0	0	0	0	0%
Other media/methods	103,000	0	0	0	0	0%
Total identification	113,000	0	0	0	113,000	11%
Customer creation						
Customer benefits, etc	0	10,000	5,000	7,000	22,000	2%
External/Internal sales	0	35,000	60,000	85,000	180,000	18%
Other media/methods	0	25,000	40,000	30,000	95,000	10%
Total creation	0	70,000	105,000	122,000	297,000	30%
Customer maintenance						
Customer benefits, etc	0	10,000	6,000	7,000	23,000	2%
External/Internal sales	0	40,000	70,000	90,000	200,000	20%
Other media/methods	0	58,000	44,000	22,000	124,000	12%
Total maintenance	0	108,000	120,000	119,000	347,000	35%
Customer upgrading						
Customer benefits, etc	0	7,000	4,000	0	11,000	1%
External/Internal sales	0	105,000	115,000	0	220,000	22%
Other media/methods	0	11,000	1,000	0	12,000	1%
Total upgrading	0	123,000	120,000	0	243,000	24%
Budget Totals						
Customer benefits, etc	10,000	27,000	15,000	14,000	56,000	6%
External/Internal sales	0	180,000	245,000	175,000	600,000	60%
Other media/methods	103,000	94,000	85,000	52,000	231,000	23%
Total budget	113,000	301,000	345,000	241,000	1,000,000	100%
% marketing budget	11%	30%	35%	24%	100%	

InterWidget Customer Results

	Prospects	*Low Boy customers*	*Good customers*	*Topper customers*	*Total*
Existing customers (start)	137	631	172	63	866
Actual fall-off	NA	88	23	3	114
Existing customers (end)	NA	543	149	60	752
Identification results	100				100
Creation results	−87	66	14	6	86
Maintenance results	NA	475	119	60	654
Upgrading results					
Upgraded to Toppers	NA	22	30	0	52
Upgraded to Good	NA	46	0		46
Total upgrade out	NA	68	30	0	98
Total upgrade in	NA	0	46	52	98
Customer results					
Prospects	151				
Customers		541	179	118	838
Customer plan					
Prospects	217				
Customers		539	174	128	841
Plan versus results					
Prospects	−66				
Customers		2	5	−10	−3
Change in percentage turnover and customers					
% turnover	NA	−7%	−4%	11%	NA
% customers	NA	−39%	12%	27%	NA

Financial analysis of InterWidget – after customer marketing

Financial analysis per customer type	*Prospects*	*Low Boy customers*	*Good customers*	*Topper customers*	*Total*
Number of prospects	151				
Number of customers		541	179	118	838
Turnover fall-off customer	NA	58,351	82,858	36,902	178,110
Turnover maintain customer	NA	647,289	857,395	1,476,060	2,980,744
Turnover upgrade out	NA	46,138	108,075	0	154,213
Turnover upgrade in	NA	0	165,715	639,626	805,341
Turnover new customer	NA	45,057	52,233	68,806	166,096
Total turnover	0	796,835	1,266,276	2,221,394	4.284,504
Costs of product actual	0	410,868	632,827	1,098,530	2,142,225
Gross margin	0	385,967	633,449	1,122,864	2,142,280
Marketing/Sales: salespeople	0	187,215	246,537	179,542	613,294
Marketing/Sales: other	113,000	121,115	114,325	67,542	415,982
Marketing/Sales: costs	113,000	308,330	360,862	247,084	1,029,276
Contribution	−113,000	77,637	272,587	875,780	1,113,004
Overheads	163,670	163,670	163,670	163,670	654,679
Pre-tax profit	−276,670	−86,033	108,917	712,110	458,325
Profit as % of sales	NA	−11%	9%	32%	11%
Marketing/Sales ROI	NA	−28%	30%	288%	45%
% Turnover	NA	19%	30%	52%	100%
% Customers	NA	65%	21%	14%	100%
% Profit	NA	−12%	15%	97%	100%

Financial analysis per customer type	*Prospects*	*Low Boy customers*	*Good customers*	*Topper customers*	*Total*
Turnover per customer	0	1,473	7,074	18,825	5,113
Margin per customer	0	713	3,539	9,516	2,556
Marketing and sales/ costs per customer	751	209	1,723	3,058	295
Contribution per customer	−751	144	1,523	7,422	1,328
Overheads per customer	1,088	303	914	1,387	781
Pre-tax profit per customer	−1,838	−159	608	6,035	547
Breakeven no. of customers	NA	662	148	43	659

Before and after comparison of results at customer level

Differences after customer marketing	*Prospects*	*Low Boy customers*	*Good customers*	*Topper customers*	*Total*
Number of prospects	14				
Number of customers		−90	7	55	−28
Turnover per customer	0	−23	28	−4,780	906
Margin per customer	0	−11	14	−2,417	461
Marketing and sales costs per customer	−1,071	−187	271	−904	−858
Contribution per customer	1,071	−185	317	1,762	748
Overheads per customer	−1	66	48	−979	93
Pre-tax profit per customer	1,072	−251	−598	431	293
Breakeven no. of customers	NA	111	35	10	−102
Profit as % of sales	NA	−17%	−9%	−8%	5%
Marketing/Sales ROI	NA	−51%	−53%	147%	22%

Before and after comparison of results at company level

Before versus after customer marketing	*Before CM*	*After CM*	*Difference amount*	*Difference %*
Number of customers	866	838	−28	−3%
Turnover	3,642,954	4,284,504	641,550	18%
Cost of product actual	1,827,571	2,142,225	314,654	17%
Gross margin	1,814,973	2,142,280	327,307	18%
Marketing/Sales: salespeople	601,950	613,294	11,344	2%
Marketing/Sales: other	396,616	415,982	19,366	5%
Total marketing/sales	998,566	1,029,276	30,710	3%
Contribution	816,407	1,113,004	296,597	36%
Overheads	596,297	654,679	58,382	10%
Pre-tax profit	220,110	458,325	238,215	108%
Breakeven no. of customers	761	659	−102	−13%
Profit as % of sales	6%	11%	5%	77%
ROI on marketing/sales	22%	45%	22%	102%

Part 3:

Your Customer Marketing Audit

Many executives have asked me this question:

> If customer marketing can deliver such a profit increase, why doesn't every company use it?

And my answer is this:

> The customer marketing strategy is quite simple. But implementing the strategy is not.

More often than not, managers underestimate the internal changes in the minds of the people and the information systems which customer marketing requires.

Have you ever been in a company when the financial administration switched over to a new computer system? Chances are that the organisation was in chaos for six months or more, despite the fact that:

- the information (financial data) was highly structured; and
- the people involved (administrators) had relatively structured ways of thinking.

In a certain sense, customer marketing means switching over to a new computer system for the marketing and sales process. And the problems are greater than those involved with a financial system because:

- the information (customer data) is not always highly structured; and
- the people involved (marketing and sales) are not always highly structured in their way of thinking and acting.

How do you know if your company is ready for customer marketing?

In our experience of working with all kinds of companies, we have come to the conclusion that there are six organisational and informational factors which are critical to the success of your customer marketing activities:

Organisational factors

1. Your customer marketing management
2. Your customer marketing staff
3. Your customer marketing logistics

Informational factors

4. Your customer marketing information
5. Your customer marketing system
6. Your customer marketing communications

To make customer marketing work for you, you have to juggle with these six factors, paying attention first to one, then to the other to avoid letting one of them fall.

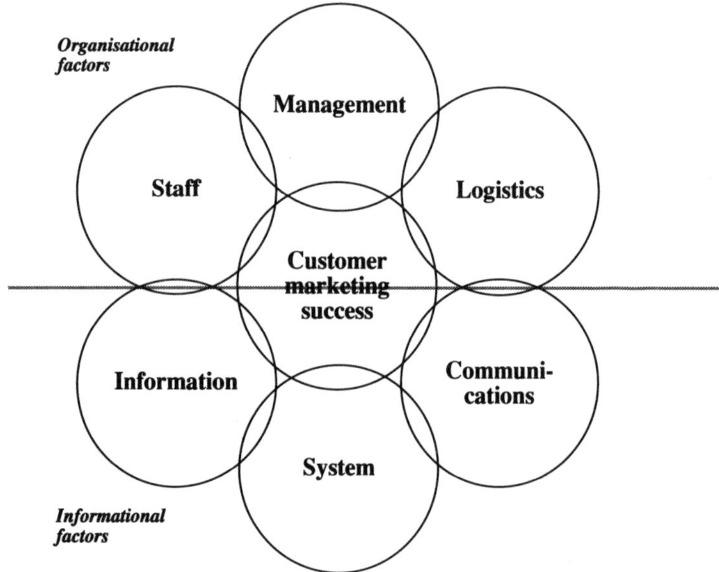

Figure 35 *Customer marketing critical success factors*

Is your company ready for customer marketing? You can learn more about these six critical success factors – and make a 'first cut' estimate of your degree of readiness – by completing this customer marketing audit.

It may take some time, and more information than you have in hand at the moment. But there is no better time to start than . . . *now*!

Customer marketing organisational factors

Customer marketing doesn't exist in a vacuum. It requires the involvement of virtually all departments in the company who must work together according to established procedures.

Now here is the organisational structure of the traditional marketing organisation, the typical line and staff 'tree' we are all familiar with.

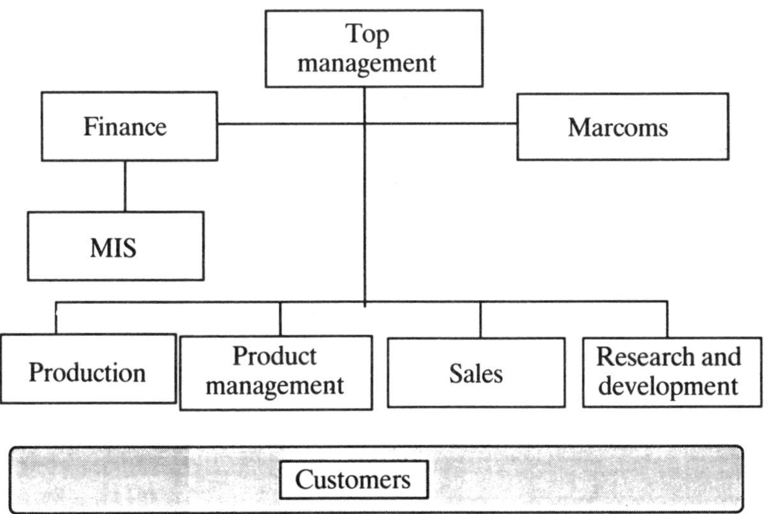

Figure 36 *Traditional marketing organisation*

Marcoms = Marketing communications
MIS = Management information systems

The organisational chart of a customer marketing organisation will probably look quite similar. After all, people have to know who their boss is. And they generally feel more comfortable working in an identifiable group.

But the way that different groups deal with customers – and each other – in a customer marketing organisation is quite different.

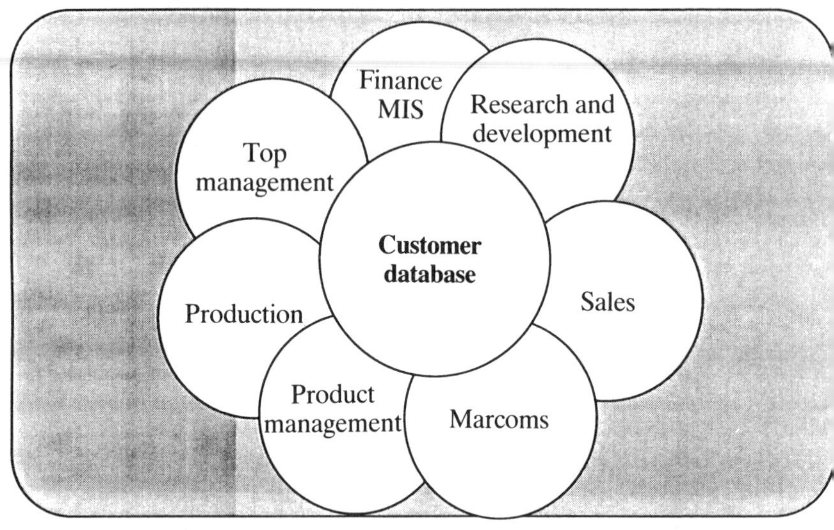

Figure 37 *Customer marketing organisation*

Marcoms = Marketing communications
MIS = Management information systems

The customer marketing organisation distinguishes itself in three ways:

1. The organisation sees itself existing surrounded by a sea of customers and prospects. Thus the organisation, and the people in it, live and breathe customers – all day long.
2. All working units are very much plugged into the customer database. Because that's where the information is which is critical to the task of the whole organisation: identifying, creating, maintaining and developing customers.
3. The working units are very much plugged into each other. Customer marketing doesn't allow time for solo-flying.

Teamwork and close coordination of tightly planned activities are required, and detailed working procedures must be worked out and followed closely.

There are two traditional areas of friction which a customer marketing organisation must solve:

- *Sales versus marketing*. It's an old story. Sales say marketing delivers lousy and poor campaigns. Marketing says sales doesn't follow up properly. Solution: give both groups customer objectives to achieve for which both are equally responsible.
- *Marketing versus EDP*. Most computer systems in companies were originally set up by the financial people – the bean counters – to keep track of accounts, send out invoices, handle the payroll. Thus the systems themselves – and the people who operate them – may not have much affinity with or interest in the marketing process, making cooperation sometimes difficult.

Now is the time to look at the organisational factors in your organisation: management, staff and logistics.

Critical Success Factor 1

Your Customer Marketing Management

Implementing (and maintaining) a customer marketing orientation in a company is not always easy. It can also require a substantial financial investment in systems, new people, training, etc. And also a lot of management time to manage the change which customer marketing brings to an organisation.

Thus customer marketing is unlikely to take hold or grow without strong management commitment to the philosophy, the activity, the process. And not just top management, but among line and staff managers throughout the organisation, because customer marketing can – and should – infiltrate every department of a company.

How do you rate your management commitment to customer marketing? Check it out! Put the appropriate score in the box.

+ = Good
0 = So-so
– = Poor
? = You don't know at this moment
NA = The item is not applicable to your organisation

Do your (top) managers:

Strategy
☐ plan the achievement of customer goals as well as financial goals?
☐ monitor customer results and take action where necessary?

Information
☐ base decisions on actual customer/prospect data?
☐ track customer satisfaction?

Budget
☐ allocate funds for customer marketing systems?

☐ allocate funds for customer orientation training?
☐ allocate time for making the organisation customer orientated?
☐ realise that creating customers requires an investment of time and money – but that the investment is the best your company will ever make?

Customer orientation

☐ phone or meet customers regularly?
☐ know if a key account is in trouble?
☐ reward sales staff on customer results as well as sales or margins?
☐ prefer to lose an order than lose a customer?
☐ ____________________
☐ ____________________
☐ ____________________
☐ ____________________

Critical Success Factor 2

Your Customer Marketing Staff

Customer marketing just won't work unless the company staff has the relevant know-how and experience, team spirit and a high degree of customer orientation.

Know-how and experience

You need a team of internal and external people with some know-how and experience in customer marketing to avoid reinventing the wheel and a costly learning curve.

Team spirit

Teamwork is also critical. Customer marketing doesn't exist in a vacuum. It requires the involvement of virtually all departments in the company who must work together according to established procedures.

Customer orientation

Customer marketing is not just a collection of methods, techniques and technologies. Customer marketing is an attitude, a way of doing business, a mentality.

You can have the most sophisticated customer marketing programme in the world – but it will fail if the customer's experience with your company doesn't reflect it.

For instance, a bank can send a lovely personal letter to current account customers suggesting they open a savings account, signed by the local bank manager. But when the customer enters the bank and is greeted by an uncaring teller who does not know – or care – about the campaign, the customer may walk out.

Customer marketing won't work until everyone shares the mentality which is reflected in a way of thinking along these lines:

> 'Our company – and my job – exists because we have customers.'
> 'We are in business to identify, make, keep and upgrade customers.'
> 'Losing a customer is bad news. Not getting him back is a tragedy.'
> 'Computer technology can help us to manage our relationships with our customers.'
> 'We should spend less time arguing with other departments and more time talking with our customers.'
> 'We will make mistakes, but a customer will forgive us if we apologise, fix the problem – and don't let it happen twice!'

How do you rate your customer marketing staff? Check it out!

+ = Good
0 = So-so
– = Poor
? = You don't know at this moment
NA = The item is not applicable to your organisation

Know-how and experience

☐ Customer marketing strategies and tactics.
Have you or your staff ever developed a customer marketing plan instead of a business plan? Allocated methods and media to reach specific customer objectives? Can you set up and operate a customer marketing programme for the sales force? And manage the overall process?

☐ Customer marketing mathematics.
Do you or your staff know how to forecast and calculate results using spreadsheets? Can they calculate marketing and sales ROI? Break-evens? Customer value? Customer lifetime?

☐ Direct marketing project management.
Many customer marketing activities and campaigns are

actually direct marketing projects which require a combination of inventiveness, creativity, entrepreneurship – and the ability to make sure that a thousand and one critical detailed steps are executed faultlessly. (Just one weak link in the chain of events, such as ordering the wrong list or a misprint on an envelope, can lose months of time and thousands of pounds.)

- ☐ Response-orientated marketing communications (internal).
  Can you or your staff brief your agency on a direct mail package or response advertisement? Can you evaluate their output? Have you worked with telemarketing agencies? Have you set up or operated an in-house telemarketing effort?
- ☐ Response-orientated marketing communications (agency?).
  Is your advertising agency committed to getting highly qualified response from direct mail and response advertising? Or are they more interested in making nice pictures, developing catchy headlines and winning prizes?
- ☐ Customer marketing systems.
  Does your MIS department have experience in developing customer/prospect database systems? If not, do they have access to outside expertise and know-how?

Team spirit

- ☐ Sales.
  Are your sales people really plugged into a customer marketing system? Do they cooperate with marketing people to improve the quality of marketing activities, lead generation programmes, etc?

- ☐ Marketing (communications).
  Are your marketing people mature enough to realise that customer marketing is not the sole prerogative of their group – but a process that requires effort, dedication and involvement from other corporate units?

- ☐ Product management.
  Do your product managers support customer marketing, or are they more obsessed with sales of (their) products?

- ☐ Finance/administration.
  Do the 'bean counters' help you to keep customer scores in addition to counting pounds and pence?

- ☐ MIS.
  Do the computer people have a special unit set up to handle (customer) marketing problems and programmes? Or are requests from marketing put on the bottom of the low priority pile?
- ☐ R&D.
  Are your R&D people plugged into customer research and other information from the customer marketing systems which can guide their development efforts? Do they go out and meet customers?
- ☐ Production.
  Are production people concerned about customer satisfaction, about high quality? Do they ever see customer satisfaction reports? Do they go out and meet happy – and unhappy – customers?

Customer orientation

How do you rate the customer orientation of these employee groups?

- ☐ Secretaries, receptionists, telephone staff
- ☐ Sales force
- ☐ Service staff
- ☐ Administration/Accounts staff
- ☐ Marketing executives
- ☐ Production crew
- ☐ Computing staff
- ☐ ____________________
- ☐ ____________________
- ☐ ____________________
- ☐ ____________________

Critical Success Factor 3

Your Customer Marketing Logistics

All too often, the best-laid marketing and sales campaigns fail because of a breakdown in marketing and sales logistics, the nuts-and-bolts details of follow-up such as despatching samples or answering requests for documentation.

But the details of marketing and sales logistics often involve direct contact with customers and prospects. Thus sloppy organisation and lack of customer orientation in this area can be very costly in terms of lost customers and prospects who decide your company doesn't really want business.

How do you rate your customer marketing logistics? Check it out!

+ = Good
0 = So-so
– = Poor
? = You don't know at this moment
NA = The item is not applicable to your organisation

☐ Database management.
Is all essential data on prospects, customers, dealers, sales force, marketing activities and products entered into the database? Is there a programme for maintaining the integrity of the data, and ensuring that changes are registered? Is security tight enough?

☐ Registration of transactions and response.
Is every customer/prospect contact registered in the database? All products or services purchased? Source code of media or marketing activity which influenced the sale?

☐ Follow-up of sales leads.
Are leads and requests for information being handled quickly and efficiently? (Try it out yourself sometime!)

☐ Order handling.
Is ordered merchandise being despatched swiftly? Services provided in time?

☐ Enquiry follow-up.
If someone requests information, a quotation, etc, will he get it within three days? And if the information will take more time to prepare, are there procedures for sending him a note or ringing him up? And what about a telephone follow-up five days after despatch to ensure that the materials arrived, and to see if you can be of more service?

☐ Invoicing.
Millions in cash flow are lost because companies can't get their statements and invoices out in time. How about your system?

☐ Complaint handling.
Do you have built-in routines for handling – and solving – complaints?

☐ Returns.
Do you handle returned merchandise effectively – not only the crediting procedures, but the inspection, restoration and handling of the goods?

☐ Chasing payment.
Does your system generate polite – but firm – reminders on overdue bills? Do you have procedures to phone the customer and discuss the problem before sending irrevocable threats of court action?

Customer marketing informational factors

Customer marketing thrives on relevant, complete and up-to-date information on your customers and prospects. This is information which you can access easily, analyse and use as the basis of personalised communications.

What is the status of your information, your system to manage it and your communications?

Critical Success Factor 4

Your Customer Marketing Information

Customer marketing can only work when you have complete and relevant information on your customers and prospects and your relationship with them. Probably you have more information than you think, but it is dispersed throughout the organisation in computers, paper files, card files and shoe boxes.

What state is your customer marketing information in? Check it out!

+	=	Good
0	=	So-so
–	=	Poor
?	=	You don't know at this moment
NA	=	The item is not applicable to your organisation

Suggestion. Make a note in the space provided by each item where the information is currently stored in your organisation.

Prospect information (leads)

☐ Complete information. ____________________
Do you register key information on your prospects: name, address, age, sex, (consumer prospect) function, company name, type of business, size (business-to-business prospect) and any other characteristics which can help you to convert the prospect to customer status?

☐ Competitive products/services. ____________________
Do you know what products and services your prospects buy from your competitors?

☐ Qualification. ____________________
Have you a way to assign a score of the probability that the prospect will become a customer?

☐ Source code. ______________________
Do you know which marketing or sales activity generated each prospect?

☐ History of relationship. ______________________
Can you easily trace the flow of (interactive) communications between you and the prospect so that you can refer to these in future contacts, or in assessing the value of the prospect?

☐ Conversion to customer. ______________________
Do you have a way to signal when, and especially the reason why, a prospect becomes a customer? Or why you lose the sale and he becomes a customer of your competitor?

Customer information

☐ Complete information. ______________________
Do you register key information on your prospects: name, address, age, sex, (consumer prospect) function, company name, type of business, size (business-to-business prospect) and any other characteristics which can help you to convert the prospect to customer status?

☐ Products purchased. ______________________
Do you keep an accurate record of what products and services your customers buy from you?

☐ Competitive products/services. ______________________
Do you know what products and services your customers buy from your competitors?

☐ Credit behaviour. ______________________
Do you track the payment and credit behaviour of your customers?

☐ Source code. ______________________
Do you know which marketing or sales activity generated each customer?

☐ Reason for buying. ______________________
Are you able to capture and store the factors which made your customer buy from you in the first place – and keep on buying?

☐ History of relationship. ______________________
Can you easily trace the flow of (interactive) communications

between you and the customer so that you can refer to these in future contacts, or in assessing the value of the customer?

Dealer/distributor information

☐ Basic company information. ____________________
Do you have complete information on your dealers and distributors as an organisation, including business history, credit checks, banking references, etc?

☐ Personal data. ____________________
Do you have complete information on the key people – not only the principals, but also the sales people, so that you can contact them personally for an incentive activity.

☐ History of relationship. ____________________
Can you easily trace the flow of (interactive) communications between you and the dealer so that you can refer to these in future contacts, or in assessing the value of the dealer/distributor?

☐ Allocated sales leads and results. ____________________
Do you register which leads you provide to your dealers and distributors, and their performance in converting the leads to solid prospects and customers?

☐ Sales achievements. ____________________
Can you easily assess how your dealers and distributors are performing for you?

Sales force information

☐ Basic personal information. ____________________
Do you have current data and background information on all your salespeople, including the phone numbers to ring when they are unreachable?

☐ Assigned clients. ____________________
Can you readily see which customers and prospects are handled by which salespeople?

☐ Allocated sales leads and results. ____________________
Do you register which leads you provide to your sales force –

and their performance in converting the leads to solid prospects and customers?

☐ Sales cycle reporting. ______
Can you quickly determine how each salesperson is progressing in his/her efforts to convert a prospect into a customer? Do you have, or need, mileposts in your sales cycle, with probability scores assigned to each step?

☐ Time accounting. ______
Can you – and the salesperson – see where and how he/she has been spending his/her time?

☐ Action planning. ______
Do you register specific activities planned for each salesperson for each account, ie visit, call for demonstration, send a business letter, etc?

☐ Sales results. ______
Does your system track sales results for each salesperson, including customer scores, ie changes in either customer status and/or prospect status caused by the salesperson?

Product information

☐ Your products and services. ______
Does your system contain data on all your products: make, models, serial numbers, prices, etc?

☐ Your competitors' products and services. ______
And similar information on key products and services of your competitors?

Marketing activities information

☐ Types of activity. ______
Does your system register all marketing activities, categorised by type, ie direct mail, response advertisement, sweepstake action, product seminar, etc.

☐ Objectives/forecast.______
Do you specify the objectives for each marketing activity – and forecast results?

- ☐ Specific media and lists employed. ____________________
  Can your system recall the media and/or lists employed for the activity so that you can use them again if they are winners – or drop them if they turn out to be losers?
- ☐ Offer made. ____________________
  Or the offer – the specific proposition designed to stimulate response so that you can use it again if it is a winner, or drop it if it is a loser?

Critical Success Factor 5

Your Customer Marketing System

Good customer marketing information is necessary. But so is a system to store, manage and analyse the information while providing tools for personalised communications.

Theoretically, your customer marketing system can be a simple card file. But with powerful personal computers costing only a few pounds a day on a lease basis, it makes sense to use one.

The basic customer marketing system structure has at its centre, of course, the customer database, with sub-databases on the sales force, marketing activities, dealers (if relevant) and products.

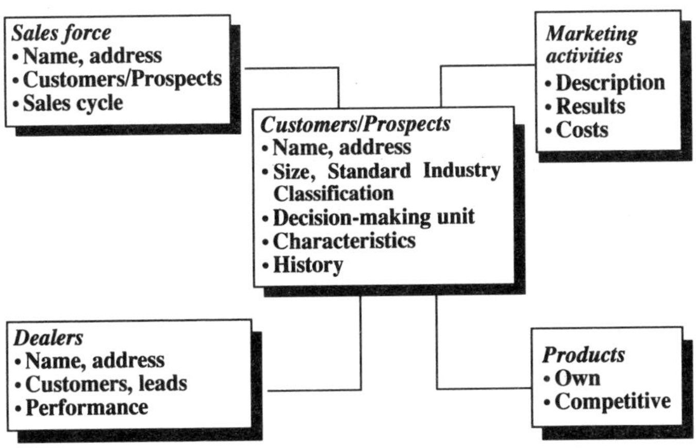

Figure 38 *Basic customer marketing system*

How do you rate your customer marketing system? Check it out!

+ = Good
0 = So-so
– = Poor
? = You don't know at this moment
NA = The item is not applicable to your organisation

Information storage and management

☐ User-friendly.
Do you need to be a rocket scientist to work with your system? Or does even the least adept salesperson discover that he/she can make call reports with the system better and faster than with pen and paper?

☐ Flexible.
Can you quickly adapt the system to meet changes in your markets and products? Or do you have to wait six months before somebody can find time to write a new program?

☐ Effective.
Does your system have the power and capacity to do all the tasks you want it to do now – and in the future?

Communications

☐ Mailings.
Can you easily send personalised mailings to prospects and customers? Which refer to your relationship (products purchased, requests for information, etc)? Look like normal correspondence (some computer systems output only in capital letters)?

☐ Telemarketing.
Does your system produce lists with telephone numbers? Can you put a telemarketing script on your computer screen so that the operator can immediately input data?

☐ Refined selections.
Can you make refined selections from your database such as: 'all customers who have spent more than £500 in the past six months, have been customers for more than three years and live within 30 miles of the store'?

Analysis

☐ Sales forecasting.
Can your system produce sales forecasts per period, per product, per salesperson, etc?

- ☐ Customer identification.
  Can your system identify your customers, not just by name and address, but also provide an analysis of customers per type and segment?

- ☐ Who buys what.
  Can your system provide an analysis of products/ services purchased by specific customer types and segments? Analysis of products purchased, customer types and segments?

- ☐ Customer value.
  Can your system provide a value for each client, ie turnover and profitability in the past, and some kind of projection for the future?

- ☐ Who decides, buys and uses our products.
  Does your system identify the 'decision-making unit' in a customer organisation – the buyers, the users, the decision makers and the influencers?

- ☐ Sales force performance.
  Does your system help you to see quickly which salespeople are performing on target?

- ☐ Distribution channels.
  Does your system help you to identify quickly which distribution channels and specific dealers/distributors are performing well?

- ☐ Media, methods and messages.
  Can your system quickly turn out an analysis of the effectiveness of key elements of your marketing activities – media, methods, messages, offers, etc?

- ☐ Return on investment.
  Can your system produce information concerning your overall return on investment from your marketing and sales efforts?

Critical Success Factor 6

Your Customer Marketing Communications

Customer marketing communications are sent out by a company to meet customer goals. As such, they must be carefully planned and targeted at specific individuals to start, maintain or renew an interactive dialogue which leads to a desired – and measurable – result.

How do you rate your customer marketing communications? Check it out!

+	=	Good
0	=	So-so
–	=	Poor
?	=	You don't know at this moment
NA	=	The item is not applicable to your organisation

☐ Personalised.
Do your communications address an individual by name? Do they appeal to his/her known needs and interests?

☐ Interactive.
Do your communications ask for some kind of response – and make that response easy through, for instance, a pre-addressed, postage-paid reply card?

☐ Benefit orientated.
Do your communications stress specific benefits that the customer or prospect will enjoy if he/she responds?

☐ Customer-orientated.
Are your routine communications (invoices, instructions, product information, etc) written for the intended receiver – or for the convenience of the sender?

Check Your Results

Go back and look at your scores and add them up.

- Do you have lots of +'s?
  Congratulations! You have a well-oiled customer marketing operation in place.
- Do you have lots of 0's?
  Why not talk to the people in the areas where there are some weaknesses to get ideas for improvement.
- Lots of –'s?
  Better make a customer marketing action plan, or accept the fact that you simply won't have a customer-orientated organisation.
- Lots of ?'s?
  Make it a point to find out these answers. Give yourself a deadline.
- Lots of NA's?
  You should really ask yourself again – 'What business am I in?'

A final suggestion: if you want to implement customer marketing in your own company, don't try to do it all at once throughout the organisation.

Start with a 'pilot project' in a small unit where you know people will be enthusiastic about trying it out, and where you are pretty sure it will be successful. Then let the pilot project participants be your ambassadors for selling the idea of customer marketing in other business units.

Further Reading from Kogan Page

Commonsense Direct Marketing, 2nd edition, Drayton Bird
Customer Service, Malcolm Peel
The Effective Use of Market Research, 2nd edition, Robin Birn
A Handbook of Sales and Marketing Management, Len Rogers
Handbook of Telemarketing, Michael Stevens
How to Market Books, Alison Baverstock
The Industrial Market Research Handbook, 2nd edition, Paul N Hague
Multi-Level Marketing, Peter Clothier
Practical Marketing, David H Bangs
Researching Business Markets, Ken Sutherland
Total Quality Marketing, John Fraser-Robinson
Understanding Brands, Don Cowley

Sales

The Best Seller, Ley D Forbes
Cold Calling Techniques, Stephan Schiffman
How to Increase Sales Without Leaving Your Desk, Edmund Tirbutt
The Sales Professional, David Mercer
Selling to Win, Richard Denny

A full list of Kogan Page business books is available from the publishers at 120 Pentonville Road, London N1 9JN.

Acknowledgements

First and foremost, we would like to thank all the members of Tyldesley Creative Writers for their enthusiasm, encouragement and submissions, including illustrations and photographs which have enabled us to produce our first anthology.

We also gratefully acknowledge the funding received from The Winkley Trust towards the cost of printing.

Finally, our thanks go to the friendly and helpful staff at Tyldesley Library.

Write from the heart

inspire-motivate-aspire-create-achieve

Tyldesley Creative Writers are members of NAWG
(National Association of Writers' Groups)

AUTHORS AND ILLUSTRATORS:

Alan F. Slater:
Here is some creative writing to share.

Anne Moores:
For me, writing is something to be delayed as long as possible. I find a close deadline and a glass (or two) of red wine very inspiring. One other thing that inspires me is going to a meeting, which always leaves me fired up to write, albeit only on tea and biscuits in this case. However, after a night's sleep I always return to my old, lazy habits.

Barbara Clark:
I like coming to the writing group because I enjoy listening to the other writers' work. Maybe I will be successful one day. I am an avid reader and always read aloud other writers' work which can be very helpful. Everyone in the group is very helpful and encouraging.

Barbara Roberts:
There's so much enthusiasm in that room when we get together. Once a month Mary gives us a topic and it's fascinating to see how differently everyone approaches it. I've realised that I can't write fiction. I can only write about something I've experienced, so that is my next challenge - to use my imagination.

Barbara Robertson:
I've been a member of the writing group for two years. In addition to learning, it is a place to meet good friends.

Diana Brooks:
I have just completed my first year at Tyldesley Creative Writers. It has been so fascinating, relaxing and friendly. The fact that I could see something in print that I have created from my own imagination has been quite motivating.

Doris Critchley:
I used to cycle and skate on ice, play tennis and ramble for pleasure. Then age took its toll on my knees so I looked for a hobby to do at more leisure. I saw an ad in the Journal for a local writing group...and that was that! As they say.

Eddie Campbell:
I am a retired English lecturer who finds creative writing a great deal more difficult than assessing the work of others but enjoys making the effort.

Ena Cunliffe:
I am an amateur WPC – writer, painter and craft person and I love it!

Gillian Whittaker:
I don't do words has been my lifelong slogan. It's the only attribute I can think of whenever I'm asked to describe myself. Staring at yet another blank piece of paper, desperately thinking of words to describe a candidate, led me to eventually ask for a transfer from Personnel to Finance and a life without words or so I hoped. Seeing the years pass by I wondered whether I ought to challenge these demons and the opportunity arose when Barbara asked me to join Tyldesley Creative Writers. I discovered that given some structure, inspiration, guidance and encouragement, I can enjoy writing and on the way home from the classes find myself smiling to myself as words just pop into my head.

Irena Gillette:
I was born in Poland and came to England in 1966. I find writing relaxing and challenging. A few years ago I joined two local writing groups. I've had three fairy tales and some of my poems published. I love nature, gardening, reading and travelling.

Jessica Kissell:
I've always enjoyed writing, therefore I like being able to showcase my work to Tydesley Creative Writers Group. I find the suggested writing topics inspirational and they always challenge my creativity. I am a distant member of the group therefore send my work through e-mail and receive feedback on the pieces I do, which helps me better myself as a writer.

Joan Patrick:
I enjoy the writing group, it keeps my brain ticking. I also enjoy meeting other people who share the same interests. When we retire, socialising is a must. I love to write humorous verse and have had a small book published entitled 'Nostalgic Titillation'.

Mary Berry:
I am very proud to be a founder member of Tyldesley Creative Writers – a fantastic group of friendly, supportive and enthusiastic people, eager to learn about the craft of creative writing. We have a great deal of fun while we learn.

Mary Morley:
Writing is a personal and private activity. It is often daunting to read your own work in public. The group offers support and encouragement and with that I am able to carry on when I think I might give it all up. It took a while for me to start writing, other commitments held me back. Now I can indulge and have

some fun, with the added bonus of the warm support of people with a common interest.

Pat Starkey:
Creative writing: my opportunity to fashion words from our fascinating language – a life-long ambition. Thought provoking, artistic, friendly and FUN!

Violet Lord:
Artist and poet.

FOREWORD

This first anthology is due to the praiseworthy foresight and endeavours of founder member Mary Berry.

Magic is a supposed, extraordinary power and quality. We hope you find enchantment in this eclectic collection of prose, poetry and pictures, which is some of the work of Tyldesley Creative Writers, for us and for you – 'The Magic of Words'.

Mary Morley
Chairman 2013

CONTENTS

THE MAGIC OF WORDS

The magic of words is important to families who care
It starts with a lullaby over the cradle, and then goes on from there
"This little piggy went to market" and all other Nursery Rhymes
Stories told on Mother's knee, and books read at bedtimes
And when our children learn to read, the seeds have already been sown
The magic carpet of the books transports them to places unknown.
We've all been there, lost in the words, oblivious to all that's around
The "Magic of Words" in the pages of books is something we're glad that we've found.

MY GARDEN

My garden is fairly nondescript
Compared to the ones next door
To my left and my right, it's a beautiful sight
Whereas mine is a bit of a bore

But I rolled up the blind this morning
And my heart was filled with a glow
'Cos my garden looked just as good as the rest
They were under a blanket of snow.

BIRTH

As every grandparent will say
The birth of our grandchild made our day.
But birth isn't just about children born
It's also about the start of the morn.
The birth of a new day.

PRICELESS OR WORTHLESS

Since the day I could fully understand my disability I began to regret that I was born. As I grew older I began to hate days and nights, for they brought nothing but anguish, desolation, as well as physical and mental suffering. Each passing day reminded me about my hopeless condition and my useless existence.

'Why was I born disabled? Why did God allow me to be the way I am?' Those questions tormented my mind, my soul and all my senses. Each night I prayed, begging to die. Yet, I kept wakening up only to be helped by the able bodies that washed me, dressed me then sat me in the wheelchair. They pushed me around from room to room, down the corridors and left me in the communal room in front of a TV. 'For what purpose I wondered? I didn't want to be here, not like this, sick, twisted and helpless.' No one could answer my questions because no one could ever read my mind... my brain was filled with personal secrets...

One day a new volunteer offered to take me out to the nearby park. The thought of seeing new surroundings made me quite excited. But, my subconscious started asking questions. 'Why me, worthless piece of human flesh..? Me, who couldn't object or agree or voice any opinion or do anything except think, listen and observe.' And as I sat strapped to my wheelchair I could only watch and ponder. I could also argue with my curious subconscious that was screaming inside my head, telling it to shut up, telling it that I wanted to go to the park, I wanted to go somewhere, anywhere...

My carer pushed my wheelchair along the pavement. It was a lovely sunny day. Spring was beaming with a new life and my head was spinning as I savoured the perfumed air. After taking me around the park my carer sat on the bench. Without saying a word he secured the brakes and started to read his paper. I watched him for a while. He probably thought that my brain was dead and didn't want to waste his time talking to someone who couldn't answer. In a way I didn't blame him. I could hear some birds arguing in the bushes and wished I could have the gift of Doctor Doolittle. My eyes wandered across the blue sky and the wispy clouds seemed to be beckoning, offering me a smoother ride. At that moment I wished that they could whisk me away into heaven and keep me there forever and ever.... Some strangers walked past carelessly, hardly noticing my presence. They all seemed to be in a great hurry as if chased by demons. Their sombre faces, faked masks absorbed by their selfish endeavours and desires. I glanced at my carer. He was engrossed in whatever he was reading as if I didn't exist. It was a pity that I did. He probably thought that I didn't have any feelings and that my brain was as green as a cabbage. I wanted to catch his attention, just to let him know that there was nothing wrong with my brain. But I couldn't do anything, just stared at him like a sheep. I felt a sudden resentment towards him, 'Why couldn't I be like him and he like me?' my subconscious questioned. 'Stop it! You can't think like this. You must apologise for your wicked thoughts.' Ashamed I

shouted at my subconscious. I felt tears welling, getting ready to drench my face. I shut my eyelids as tight as I could. I didn't want him to see me cry but I couldn't control them. At that moment I felt someone stroking my hand. As I opened my eyes I saw a little boy with an angelic face standing before me.
"Mummy, tell me why is this man crying?" His childish voice sounded like music to my ears. 'Man, he called me man.' I wanted to thank him for his kindness but instead of the words a few bubbles popped out from the corner of my drooling mouth.
"Don't waste your time lad, he doesn't speak and doesn't understand anything," my carer told him then carried on reading.
"Mummy look, he can blow bubbles."
His mother blushed, "I am very sorry, my son is not old enough to understand," and pulling him gently away from the chair added, "Jude, I think that the man does understand and wanted to say thank you for stopping by." She smiled at me a radiant smile and I blinked.
"Mummy, why he looks different from us...?"
"My dear Jude, you're asking too many questions."
"But Mummy, last night you told me that I was priceless, is this man priceless too?"
"Of course he is. In God's eyes this man is as priceless as you are and as everyone else because God loves us all. We're all his children no matter how we look."
I watched them walking away. My heart leapt when Jude turned around and waved. My carer finished reading, got to his feet and wheeled me back to my safe haven. As I gazed at the sky I could see Jude's angelic face in every cloud and his mother's beautiful words kept ringing in my head like crystal bells.

WISHFUL THINKING

He said he would write –
was he just being kind?
We've both left our youthful years behind.
He seemed so honest –
I believed all he said.
Could it be the desire
Was all in my head?
At last! There's the postman –
I know his rat-a-tat
Praise be! A letter lies on the mat.
Eagerly I read it – but, alas
It's just another advert for gas!

THE ONE-EYED DONKEY

A little Cyprus donkey
Was kicked and left to die.
His owner had abandoned him
'cause he only had one eye.

But the sanctuary soon found him
And brought him home to live.
He had a quirky character
And a lot of cheek to give.

They called him Guy and treated him.
They tried to heal his sight.
But his eye was badly damaged
And never would be right.

Another donkey joined him soon
They said her name was Vi.
Also, coincidentally,
She only had one eye.

When Guy and Vi stood side by side,
They shared their faulty sight.
Guy could cover all things left
And Vi saw all things right.

They got on well and soon enough
Young Simon came along,
A donkey babe – his sight was checked
And there was nothing wrong.

The following year, young Di was born.
She too had normal sight.
At last, a perfect family,
Now everything was right.

So Guy and Vi and Si and Di
Were happy to agree
That the sanctuary in Cyprus
Was the ideal place to be.

When Guy looked round at Donkey Field,
He gave a happy sigh.
There was no disadvantage
To having just one eye.

FRONTLINE

Soldiers, obeying commands, in distant lands.
News reports, optimistic.
Family and friends broken in grief.
Comrades in arms in disbelief,
Bearing the casket.
Miltary Honours.
Union Jack.
Another man injured, taking the flack.
Shot down.
Blown up.
Maimed.
Mentally scarred.
Yet still they dare.

MY SPECIAL DAY

"Is this next train on time do you know?"

"Should be, although you never can be sure this time of day, rush hour you know."

"Yes I know. Not used to travelling so early in the day."

"Well it could be leaves on the line, wrong kind of snow or points failure."

"Oh dear, well let's hope it's on time for my connection. I need to be at Piccadilly for 10 a.m."

"I am sure you will be fine. Is it a day out?"

"Yes it is a day out, looked forward to it for a while now."

"London?"

"Yes London – for the day."

"For the day, well I hope you enjoy it. Will you be doing anything special?"

"Yes, you could say that. I will meet friends when I get there."

"Lovely. That's a big box you are taking with you."

"I know but it's necessary I'm afraid."

"Oh well, here's the train now, it's usually a bit of a crush so hang on to your box."

"Yes I will and it's been nice talking to you. Have a good day!"

"Afraid it's just the usual nine to five for me today, desk and phone in the city. I feel I have to ask you though, why carry such a big box for just the day."

"Well, it's my hat for the garden party at Buckingham Palace this afternoon and I don't think it would have looked quite right to wear it just now on the train."

"I DON'T DO WORDS !"

"I DON'T DO WORDS !"……

Certainly not those describing things, those things that can fill a page, those things that I can never grasp and that desert me whenever I need them.

"I DON'T DO WORDS !"……

Whether it's because I wasn't given my share or whether I've mislaid them somewhere. Maybe they just got bored, fed up of listening to music, being jumbled up by all that dancing, and left, decided to go somewhere they'd feel more useful.

"I DON'T DO WORDS !"……

I may have had some before the English teacher uttered those terrifying WORDS "and now composition". I think she really really scared them and they've gone away. AWOL, Underground. If I concentrate I think I can hear them squeaking, hiding just behind my ears.

"I DON'T DO WORDS !"……

Especially not big evocative descriptive WORDS that encapsulate the moment, you know, those succinct WORDS. Sometimes a little doing WORD will squeeze out unexpectedly and surprise everyone. Where did that come from? I'm sure it must have some friends who would like to express themselves instead of being restrained. Maybe they are being bullied by bigger more important WORDS that carry more weight like transcendentalism.

"I DON'T DO WORDS !"……

I would explain to prospective employers. I can do numbers I insisted although to be fair I can't add up, multiply, or heavens forbid, divide. I can take away a bit. Do you mean subtract? someone once pointed out. Oh yes that's the WORD I'm looking for.

"I DON'T DO WORDS !"……

Sometimes I try to act casual, nonchalant, pretending I don't really need a WORD. Hoping to catch the pesky things off guard. I can sense that they are there but they are so nimble, like lightning. As soon as I try to find one they disappear. Who knows where to? That big thesaurus in the sky maybe? There's definitely some in the "iCloud" because I put some there once when I had an inspired moment.

"I DON'T DO WORDS !"…..

Sometimes they like to have a bit of fun and transpose letters, much to the amusement of my friends who have become adept at translating to baffled strangers. It's a sort of cross between Stanley Holloway, Esperanto and Norman Collier as the WORDS tumble out.

"I DON'T DO WORDS !"……

I explained to Barbara as she invited me to join the Creative Writing group. It must have been quietly, because the next minute she'd picked me up and was transporting me to Tyldesley. Never mind I thought, I can have a cup of coffee, a biscuit, and listen to everyone else exhibiting their WORDS. I couldn't believe how much I enjoyed myself, listening to wonderful imaginative pieces but just as I began to relax IT happened. Mary asked us to write something about the Magic of WORDS. I don't do WORDS I wanted to wail but how could I, I was at Creative Writing. Oh well, it was nice while it lasted. I'm sure no one will notice if I don't turn up again.

But then, on the way home, reflecting on the fun we'd had that night, I suddenly thought maybe I could manage just a little WORD.

DUST ON THE MARMALADE

Way back in the old days of variety shows, touring was par for the course. You would do a show one week in Bradford, the following week in Brighton and the third week in Glasgow. So it went on, all through the year, punctuated by Christmas pantomimes in the cities and summer seasons at the seaside. In a similar vein in the 1980's, 1990's and beyond, Roy and I were touring with 'The Ken Dodd Happiness Show'. We got quite a feel for the large and small hotels and travel lodges up and down the country. It was therefore, without a second thought, that we booked accommodation at a small Scottish hotel when we were doing a show in Falkirk.

We arrived at the hotel at about 6.00pm. and as the show started at 7.30pm. we just had time to drop off our bags and collect the key. This was because all Doddy shows finish quite late, so no small hotel is going to stay open and wait for us. The door was answered by a sour faced, baggy-trousered old man who would have looked more at home behind a farm tractor. We asked for a key and told him the reason but he said the door was always bolted at 11.00pm and no way was he going to change that rule. As there was no chance of us finding other accommodation at such short notice we practically got on our knees to beg for the key. After what seemed like hours, he gave one to us then shuffled away muttering under his breath.

After the show, we arrived back at the hotel slightly earlier than usual as we weren't sure whether 'Farmer Giles' would go back on his word and bolt the door. To our delight he didn't, so we crept in using our torch which we always carried. There was an instant smell of scones which we always think is suspicious when there is no baking going on! A mountain of coats hung in the hall – all seemingly suspended from one hook, and they all seemed to be stuck together.

We entered the bedroom with trepidation and were right to do so. The old cracked fireplace had a pile of rubble in the grate. The iron railings on the bed seemed to be caving in. The flock mattress was moulded to a pit in the middle and there was no way you could stay on the edge. The grey sheet and the 1940's eiderdown were no compensation. There was a jug in a bowl on the rickety dresser. The water in the jug was discoloured. Was it water??? I looked under the bed just in case there was a body there – but all I found was dirty oilcloth and what looked like builders' rubble and, unsurprisingly, a badly stained potty. The room obviously wasn't en suite so I reluctantly crept to the bathroom. I could hardly get in because of the presence of a broken washing machine topped by a jam jar full of greasy plastic flowers.

After a night in the 'pit' we got up earlier than usual as the incentive was just to get out. We didn't want breakfast, but felt we had to eat something as there weren't many eating places open in Falkirk on an early Sunday morning in the 1980s. In the lounge we sat on slashed black imitation leather seats beside a long low coffee table which was set for breakfast. The chipped ugly green cups were face down on the cracked saucers. The almost burnt toast looked as though it had been there for a week and the HP sauce bottle had a very congealed lid. In the middle of the table was an old glass dish full of marmalade. There was a hard film on top of it and there was dust on the film. I was staring at this when 'the lady of the house' appeared. She was a personification of the establishment she was running. She was old and toothless and wore an absolutely filthy denim apron. 'Will you be wanting a cooked breakfast?' she asked, and we both said 'No' far too quickly. In the end we settled for boiled eggs but they were watery and we couldn't trust the toast to mop them up.

We escaped as soon as we could and by mid morning we were well on our way to our next venue at Inverness. We would have reported the Falkirk hotel but felt that as the owners were so old and incompetent it wouldn't be long before the place closed down anyway. Although the dining at Falkirk was not good - because we have a sense of humour - we were able to 'dine out' on our experience there for many years to come.

MY MAKEOVER

I really must sort out my image,
I'm hoping to get a new me.
I'll find one of those plastic surgeons,
Who'll restore my elasticity.

Maybe I'll have my face Botoxed,
Then have coloured streaks in my hair.
Get a tattoo on the back of my neck,
Make my bosoms a much bigger pair.

Have studs in my face and my navel,
Get my flabby bits lifted and tucked.
Have a massage in one of those parlours,
Then I'll need my lipo to be sucked.

I don't know if I can afford it,
But I do know there's someone who can.
And if the old beggar starts moaning,
I'll buzz off and get a new man.

DIAMONDS ARE FOREVER

Sleeping, dreaming; developing
I was snug and warm in my cocoon; a womb of ancient rock
Then ripped from my roots by menacing mining machines
Disturbed, disrupted and elevated into the bright sunlight
My protective marquisette shell shattered and I lay bare
Naked; revealing my breathtaking beauty
Brilliantly reflecting the rays of the sun
Flawless, clear and perfectly pure
Contrasting starkly with the faulty stones that simultaneously surfaced
To the sense of sight as the sound of the clearest tinkling silver bell to the ear
Experienced hands cut and crafted; experts faceted and polished
Designers of distinction fashioned my shape to decorate a royal skin
I sparkled; outshone the lesser gems in the multi coloured choker
The warm satin pearls reflected my brightness
I put the fire into the rich red rubies
The glint into the glass green emeralds
And illuminated the blue of the darkest sapphires
In response, they lent me their light, reflecting a kaleidoscope of colour
I reigned, magnificent; a jewel of merit,
Photographed, catalogued, and listed in record books
Famous for my perfection
A diamond outliving the royal necks I've adorned

GOOD WITH WORDS

It may be inelegant and hackneyed but the expression, 'he or she is good with words', is meant to be the ultimate compliment to those who are able to combine a broad vocabulary with an aptitude to use it effectively.

Who worthier of the accolade than Oscar Wilde, who used the English language lavishly and to such great effect, to adorn his poetry, his plays and his inimitable witticisms? Politicians too are good with words, skilled practitioners of rhetoric as a means of persuading us of their infallibility despite overwhelming evidence to the contrary.

But consider for a moment those who are not particularly good with words, but who nonetheless are able to express themselves with just one word. They are the masters of verbal minimalism and could be said to be 'good with words'.

You see, there are many instances where people of a certain ilk, either collectively or individually, become inexplicably attracted to a particular word and insist on using it at every available opportunity.

For example, the word 'diabolical' once swept through the footballing fraternity like a second visitation of the plague. Managers, players and supporters would use it with complete abandon as if were a symbolic imperative of their allegiance to the great game and set them apart from the common herd. The pitch was diabolical, the ref was diabolical and the players were diabolical to a man. Somehow Diablo the devil had inveigled himself into every aspect of the game. The effect was contagious and became likened to an endemic disease. The chief medical officer warned that even a mild dose of 'Rooneyitis' could quickly develop into a full blown case of 'Lexicum Diabolica' and recommended fingers in ears for

those in the vicinity of an outbreak.
At an individual level my uncle Jim, was besotted with the word ‘actually’ and would sometimes use it ten or fifteen times during the course of conversation with my parents. My sister and I used to secretly log the frequency of usage on jotting pads. When he left, we would spend ages mercilessly mocking him and repeating the word to each other with grossly exaggerated affectation.
“Actually” we would say, “well actually”, “I actually think I should stop saying actually but actually I just can’t help it.”
He became known affectionately as ‘Uncle Actually’.
My aunt Marjory on the other hand had an obsession with a word, ‘ridiculous.’ Everything was positively ridiculous.
“I caught a train to Hull yesterday” she once said, “I had to contend with this ridiculous little ticket clerk.”
“Would you like a return ticket madam?” he asked.
“Well of course I would.” I retorted. “What a ridiculous question. Who would want to stay in Hull?”
Personally, I don’t like the word one bit. As a word I think it is quite....well actually quite ridiculous.

OFFICE GOSSIP: FIRST TEA BREAK

Jade & Angela
"I don't know what they think I am. This is just sooooo not within my remit and definitely not in the job description. I think they've got a nerve. I'm gonna ring me manager and have it out with her. It really needs sortin' out."

"I know I agree with you, they want every last drop you can give!"

Sue
"Called in Aldi last night – got a bottle of cheap wine and a ready meal.
It was good, can't complain, ate it whilst watching 'Corrie' then fell asleep."

Cathy
"Oh, you're lucky. Kids were creating all night, Our Tracey wants new trainers, Charmaine wants her nails done and our Wayne, well he just sits there with his mobile phone textin' all't time!"

Merle
"Oh they drive you mad – nails done at 13, I'd only just found out what a nail file were for when I turned 13. Anyway our Joanne wants a tattoo – I said you can forget about that lady, you are far too young and who's going to pay for it?.....and anyway if you're not 18 they want your parent's consent.

"I phoned our Jean I told her I am sick of these kids, they're drivin' me mad."

Annette
"Oh kids are least of my problems – I told you didn't I that I was going to follow Andy on Sunday, - I kept sayin' I would, well I was right – he is havin' an affair. I'm devastated – don't know what I'm gonna do. Should I let him know that I know?"

Winnie
"Lorraine had to have that operation on her back, she was in so much pain, sent her a card from us all, hope she's soon back. Poor love!

"And…….Marie who left last week, well she says her new job is goin' just fine. I think she's glad she left even though it wasn't any more money."

Sophie
"Hey, do you like this blouse or do you think it's too loud? I love it but I'm not sure it goes with this skirt. I've kept me boots on today cause it's bloody cold out there.
And………you know what, that lad who I've had my eye on on the bus – well this morning he winked at me. He looks a bit like Harry out of One D. I can't believe no one has snapped him up already. Anyway you never know he might speak tomorrow, he's gorgeous."

Sue
"Best get summat done…it's half past 9."

A SHOCKING ACCIDENT

This is a tragic story containing sporadic rhyming lines, with random and abrupt changes in meter and style, for which the writer offers his profuse apologies.

The Snodbury village postman's name was Ben
And he'd done the job since only God knows when
To say he was a ladies' man would be rather euphemistic
For his collar, his jacket, his tie and his boots were always smeared with lipstick.

Harold Fishwick had long suspected that Ben
Did dalliance with Gladys, his wife, now and then
And it hadn't gone unnoticed that Harold's son Fred
Had a great mop of hair that was Post Office red

Now Harold had often been heard to say
The time would come when the postman would pay
For turning the head of dear Gladys, his wife
Which with VAT, may amount to Ben's life

It was on that sunny April day
That Ben was seen to make his way
With his usual nonchalant charm
And a parcel tucked under his arm
Up the path to the door of the Fishwick's home
Where hung a brass knocker the size of a gnome

Ben brushed his hair in hope of greeting Gladys with a smile
He had this great propensity for putting on the style
Then reaching for the knocker on Harold Fishwick's door

With one faint cry he fell there and lay prostrate on the floor
One knock was heard within the house, one final fleeting knock
When Gladys Fishwick answered it she got a dreadful shock

O Harold dear, the postman's here, he's lying on the floor
His boots appear to be on fire, he's not done that before
The knocker's melted off the door and fallen on his head
He doesn't look so well at all, I think he could be dead
Well bless my soul said Harold he looks thoroughly deceased
We'd better send for someone, like a doctor or a priest

Doing his rounds at that time of day was Syd
The sharp eyed local copper
Who came to investigate what he believed
Were the tell-tale signs of a stolen knocker

`Ello, `ello, `ello he said what's goin` on `ere then
Kippin` whilst on duty, that's not like postman Ben
I could book the man for loiterin` with intent, he said
If it weren't for the fact, by the look of `im,
That the man's completely dead

I'll send for Shylock Homes our chief detective
His techniques have never failed to be effective

You can't touch me said Harold, I'm too important round here
I'm the chairman of the ferret club and a car-park overseer

You won't be that important when they bang you up in jail
The way you're treated there mate will be a different tale

The Magic of Words

It'll be Fishwick, stitch them mail-bags
And Fishwick, break them rocks
And Fishwick, shave that silly beard
And wash your flippin` socks

Said Harold, who's this Shylock Homes,
I've never come across him
I suppose he's like the rest of you cops,
Size twelve boots and exceedingly dim

You've never heard of Shylock Homes?
He's brilliant for starters
He'll find the clue that points to you
And `ave your guts for garters

Now Shylock was a dapper man
White gloves, cravat and yellow shoes he wore
He spotted an electric cable
Hanging from the back of Fishwick's door
What do we have here then, what stories could this tell?
Said Harold, That's just a cable from the old electric bell

It's Shylock Homes you're dealing with not some stupid bobby
I know the efficacy of electricity, electrics is my hobby
You wished this man to snuff it, you caused this man to die,
By connecting up the knocker to the mains supply

At this, Gladys quickly arose from her chair
I really do think that is terribly unfair

My Harold didn't do it, he hasn't got the skill
He couldn't even fix the fuse on his electric drill

I know he didn't do it, he hasn't got the knowledge
He doesn't know what day it is, he's never been to college

Now all sit down said Gladys, I'll switch to radio two
And we'll listen to some music whilst I go and make a brew
The music soothed the tension and they all began to hum
With Harold playing on the spoons and Shylock on a makeshift drum

Let's drink champagne said Harold, his manner beginning to soften
I'll drink to that all day said Sid; we should do this far more often

Gladys by now was recapturing her youth
Dancing with Shylock the dapper young sleuth
Sid doffed his helmet, swept Harold away
And danced what they thought was the Paso-doble

Then the music stopped abruptly and the jollity abated
An announcement was to come so they stood in awe and waited

It has come to our attention as I'm just about to mention
That the Met Office has issued this dire warning
That a freakish bolt of lightning of magnitude quite frightening
Struck Snodbury at ten o'clock this morning

Also professor DC Spark
Has issued this profound remark

The current squared created by the voltage generated

Times the sum of the resistance from the ether to the floor
Gave the power that was needed and in this case was exceeded
To melt the average knocker off the average front door

Shylock stood at six foot four and pointed sadly at the door
Alas he said we must consent this was a shocking accident.

OLYMPICS 2012

Passion, adrenaline – burning in his eye;
A Reflection of the flame,
Light – pouring from the sky,
Providing power; energy ready for the game.

A crystal bead trickles,
A perfect path down his cheek.
A silent splash, a signal,
His posture, a faultless physique.

So much time now feels so little,
Make or break,
Affirm the committal,
3, 2, 1…

So strong,
Can't go wrong,
The world, now a silent bubble.

Surreal is time,
Focused on the line,
And already it is over.

A cheer from me, my mother, my brother,
My foe, my friend we commend together.
The country, we all re-unite,
As one big team, just for the night.

Passion, victory – flecks of gold in his eye;
A Reflection of the medal.
Light beaming from the sky,
Proud.

HOT BUTTERED TOAST (1)

I happily recall the delights of autumn in the nineteen fifties. Scuffing through the leaves in the park. The orange globules of light mistily hanging from the gas lamps. Arriving home at five o'clock just as the curtains are being drawn. The tea is brought in a fat brown teapot and the butter is melting in a saucer on the hearth. The purring cat is cosily curled up on the rug.

What a contrast to high summer on foreign shores where the sun shines boringly all of the time.

Mum toasts a thick slice of white bread on a toasting fork. The fire is warm and comforting, casting jumping shadows over the dimly lit room. I revel in the luxury of my arm chair and delight at being spoiled as the hot buttered toast is handed to me.

Moments like this are priceless.

MOMENTS OF PRECIOUS PEACE

I
The alarm clock is unset and silent.
In natural wakefulness yet in dreamlike doze
I stare at the sky and it becomes part of my blue room.
Wrapped in my nest of duck down and feathers
I fly among the clouds.

II
The window pane prevents me touching
the Clematis outside.
Its flower, saucer sized and pink,
sways in May's breeze.
Birds sing and chatter in their nesting place,
their chicks rocked to sleep in dense trees
hidden safe from the tabby with a grinning face.

III
A walk beside the river Eden,
its movement slow and ringed with drops of rain.
Through Cumbrian fields of Kirkby Stephen
where wet grass shines my boots again
and ewes, in tatty woollen coats, graze contentedly
as their lambs butt ferociously at the source of milk.
Afraid to be alone, they huddle in a bunch
or follow and gambol on legs of spring
towards the water's edge
and I digest with guilt the recent Sunday lunch.

IV
The peace of silence as it falls gently in the night

mingled with snow so glistening white
that the hibernating garden gleams,
lit by moonlight, silver-bright
and I am warm and safe from winter's frosty bite.
I notice the morning's tell tale tracks
of a bird's hunt for food,
then the heavier prints of that prowling cat.
Our homes and cars like igloos.

ALL TICKETS SOLD

Mi Dad watched Wanderers years and years followed them hail rain or snow
"They're our Team always have been, through thick & thin y'know"
They changed the managers, changed their Team always tryin' to be "On the Ball"
Up n'down the Divisions – riding high and winnin' – or an end of season "fall"

Saturday Bus took them to Burnden big queue for it outside Temperance Bar
There were Harry, Fred, Phil and Bill, once they got on sharra it wasn't far.
They'd talked last week's match to death – how Lofthouse had saved the day
Gettin' through that tackle, down't left wing – Marvellous!! What do you say?

Then….. One season they did it, they won and Wembley were in sight.
I'll tell you they were so excited they couldn't sleep at night.
Wembley tickets went on sale and they formed an orderly queue one night in't cold
Only to find that when they got to front hopes were dashed, all tickets had been sold.

Many years later there were talk of Wanderers getting a new ground
Mi Dad thought this were crazy – surely nowhere better could be found
"They'll never leave Burnden it's an institution, Nay - never fear.
Where? Middlebrook, Horwich, who's gooin' go and watch em up there?"

A CHRISTMAS STORY

The wind echoed like a whispered melody as it danced amongst the trees. Audible yet out of sight, a choir of bats, crickets and owls played harmony to the melody. The sweet sounds helped subdue his bitterness and his heavy, harsh footsteps softened. He couldn't be angry out here; sad but not angry. He started to reminisce but was soon distracted by silver sparkles flickering in front of him, just visible between the trees. Half a minute later he was no longer protected by the distractions of the forest, but stood exposed to the lake. The row boat he once knew to be red, bobbed along the edge of the lake. He stepped slowly and cautiously towards the water before kneeling down. Cold, sharp water droplets pricked his face like a thorn warning him to stay away, he thought, but he had no choice.

Half way across the lake and the cottage could be seen much clearer now. He placed his oars carefully back inside the boat and just drifted, procrastinating his arrival. With forced, steady breathing he slipped his right hand into his coat pocket and retrieved the scrunched up letter, damp from the splashes of water. He unfolded it then re-read it.

Dear Cole,

I am writing to push you for a response regarding the proposal presented to you in my previous letter. I understand that the implications and responsibilities, at times, will be very demanding but considering your family history in the business, I trust you have the skills and abilities to cope making you perfect for the position.

I also felt the need to inform you of your father's current condition, which unfortunately is slowly, but indeed, deteriorating. Based on this, your father and I would appreciate your reply as soon as is possible therefore hope to see you at the family cottage at 11pm on the 24th of this month.

I look forward to seeing you, as does your father.

Yours sincerely,

Roger Elfen

A mixture of emotions once again spun around his body. He was annoyed that his father couldn't have spared any time to write himself rather than his assistant doing so. However, the news of his father's condition sparked regret as Cole acknowledged what it had had to come to before he agreed to meeting him. His father's work always came first for as long as he could remember and although Cole knew his father was doing work for a good cause, he was always saddened by the little amount of time spent with him. This was, of course, except for 5 days every July which his father called a 'mid-year break' spent at the family cottage in Canada, one of his father's favourite places and far away from where they lived. These times were his fondest memories. Cole permanently moved to Canada at the age of 19 in hope of finding a career and life for himself away from the assumed career path set out for him by his father which inevitably caused a long lasting quarrel between the two. Now his father wanted to meet at the family cottage to discuss business.

A thud startled Cole as the boat hit solid ground. His attempt to procrastinate his arrival failed due to the wind, which now seemed to be fluttering around inside his stomach as well as the trees. Before he knew it, he was standing in front of the cottage. A mixture of dust and dirt coated the windows, preventing him from seeing anything more than a warm golden glow, illuminating the sparkly wreath hung carefully from the paint peeled front door – a tell-tale sign that his father had already arrived. Surprisingly, the old door didn't creek as Cole leant down on the door handle pushing it open.

"Nicholas, Cole is here!" Roger shouted in the direction of the kitchen just before greeting Cole himself.

A big man walked in from the kitchen and towards Cole. His expression was buried under locks of white curly hair covering his face, also hiding any evidence of his 'deteriorating condition', as Roger called it. A husky voice spoke:

"Son, I'm delighted you could make it." He paused to clear his throat, letting slip a loud, chesty cough which calmed into a quieter rumble before allowing him to continue. "I'm getting too old now, you see. I need someone to take over. If you don't, there's no one left. Millions of people will be left disappointed, men, women, children, without my services…"

"You will accept the proposal, won't you Cole?" Roger interrupted, anxious to prevent Nicholas from getting too worked up. Ignoring Roger, he resumed,

"I was too work consumed, I lost sight of myself and my own family but you won't be that way, you'll be much better than I was."

Cole couldn't deny that the job would be incredible but the risk of being like his father and pushing aside his family was what he always wanted to avoid.

"Come," his father commanded, leading the way outside and around to the side of the cottage.

Blue, red, green, yellow, orange, purple; Cole squinted as an explosion of colour ignited in front of him. He felt the magic of it all tingle through his body and happiness and joy began to take over, making it harder and harder for him to think. Despite years of building a different life for himself, he could feel it now clearer than ever, that this is what he was meant to do. His father reached for his hat and pulled it off revealing more locks of snow white hair. With the hat in his hand, he extended his arm towards Cole whilst bursts of colour still danced above them. Cole reached out his arm, meeting his father's and clutched the hat gingerly. Placing it upon his head, the agreement was done and the proposal accepted.

His father – Father Christmas, chuckled with glee.
The hat passed on, down another generation of the family tree.
Retirement could be enjoyed with knowledge Christmas would be again filled with happiness from presents under the tree.

HOT BUTTERED TOAST (2)

Tiptoe unto the door,
The paint peeling,
Bare feet frozen on the floor.

Eyebrows lift, eyes widen.

Peering in, she sees no sign,
But a glimpse, a reflection,
Of a memory only to remind.

Eyes shut, wrinkles tighten.

Panic spreads upon her chalk white face,
Slamming the door, now nothing to illuminate.
She cannot wait.

Coat on, door shut.

Icy wind, hammering her face,
Her footsteps brisk,
Hair blown out of place.

Warmth. In she struts.

High on the shelves,
Twinkling like a star,

The glistening gold foil, attracts her from afar.

Eyes lift, face brightens.

Icy wind, now a cool breeze,
Her footsteps light,
Home with her package and at ease.

Eyebrows lift, eyes lighten.

Pop.

She peels the foil back,
'Mmm', she mutters,
A morning wouldn't be complete without,
Her 'Toast and butter!'

GRASS

I went for a walk up in Scotland last week,
I called it a little adventure.
A farmer talked to me whilst shearing his sheep,
He showed me a ram with a denture.

The ram was a prize one, he ate loads of grass,
But sometimes sheep's teeth become worn.
That's what happened to Samson, he went on a fast
And stood there and looked all forlorn.

The vet had a ponder then sorted him out
With a set of false teeth that looked great.
Now they can't grow enough grass for Samson the ram,
And he won the first prize at the fete.

KISSED BY A BREEZE

Long beach lay at my feet, a golden band
Lit by heavenly star, high in the sky
Breeze kisses my face, refreshes my mind

With powerful sunrays, life giving hand
Warming up the sea, brightening up day
Long beach lay at my feet, a golden band

Sand meeting ocean sky embracing land
Seagulls crying overhead, chasing sunray
Breeze kisses my face, refreshes my mind

Horizon and heaven, were they planned?
Waves corroding coast line, my cosy bay
Long beach lay at my feet, a golden band

Kelp and seashells adorn the golden sand
Sunrays ride wild horses day after day
Breeze kisses my face, refreshes my mind

Neptune raises his trident in right hand
Lightning rips the sky makes the ocean sway
Long beach lay at my feet, a golden band
Breeze kisses my face, refreshes my mind

A FOGGY AFTERNOON

Market Street, Manchester, Wednesday afternoon, 20th November 1935. Miss Elise Matthews hurried out of Dolcis shoe shop where she had worked as First Sales for the past two years. The Wednesday half day off was very welcome as she worked long hours, including Saturdays, and she had a ten mile journey home.

The fog had been hanging over the city all morning and threatened to take over the afternoon and evening. Sometimes, on her half day, she would stay and see a film or a matinee at one of the theatres but today she just wanted to get home.

At the railway station she got as near as she could to the fire in the ladies waiting room. She met up with her friend Dora who worked at Affleck and Brown's department store. They both had a good moan about the fog.

The train ride was long and slow but eventually she arrived at Tyldesley. The last part of her journey would take her down a long lane and across a field to her home at Meanley Farm Cottage. The fog was getting ever thicker. Obviously she was familiar with the route home but today she became disorientated and completely lost. She couldn't see her hand in front of her face and every step was tentative. It was eerily quiet so it wasn't surprising that she screamed when she heard a sudden noise.

"Miss, stop!" said a man's voice and she felt a hand on her shoulder. "Don't move or you'll be in the pond."

He guided her back to the footpath and pointed her in the right direction. He was a miner coming home from the nearby pit.

“I know this route backwards – even in this pea souper. You were nearly a gonner then”.

Elise gratefully thanked him and carefully continued her walk home.

The following Wednesday Elise made the same journey home but in much brighter conditions. Coincidentally she met the same miner in the same spot by the pond. He wasn’t a bad looker, this knight in shining armour. A new romance started which blossomed into marriage.

Elise never ever moaned about foggy days again.

BIRTHS, MARRIAGES AND DEATHS

These columns are a staple element of local newspapers but they are mere announcements and behind the information given possibly lie interesting stories. I have selected a few of these announcements from the Coldstone Journal and a few newspaper articles from the Daily Comet which perhaps throw some intriguing light on these announcements.

COLDSTONE JOURNAL March 5th 1950

Mr and Mrs Josiah Sleight are pleased to announce the birth of a son, Josiah on 29th February at home in North Avenue.

DAILY COMET 2nd March 1950

Milkman Tim Delivers Pintas and Baby

When Mrs Josiah Sleight went into labour unexpectedly, she was alone at home. Luckily, milkman Tim Handy heard her cries as he deposited the usual two pints on her doorstep. He pushed the door open and found Mrs Sleight lying on the floor. He quickly realised what was happening, assumed the role of midwife and delivered a bouncing baby boy.

"I was a boy scout," said Tim, "so I'm always prepared. Also my ferrets had some young ones recently so I knew exactly what to do."

Tim certainly lived up to his name, Handy by name, handy by nature.

Later the proud father said that he and his wife had agreed to call the baby Josiah Timothy in appreciation of the milkman's help. "It's appropriate," he said, "particularly as young Jos has red hair just like Tim's."

COLDSTONE JOURNAL 3d September 1975

Sleight - Astley The marriage took place at St Swithin's Church between Josiah Timothy Sleight and Vera Elspeth Astley on Saturday 29th August . Congratulations from both families. Honeymoon in Skegness.

DAILY COMET 5th September 1975

Rugby League Star Weds

Coldstone Cougars were without their star winger, Jos Sleight on Saturday as he was taking part in another match to vivacious Vera Astley. "Apart from it being my wedding,"said speedy, elusive Jos, "I wasn't really fit enough to play. The lads took me out on a stag do on Friday night and either I had one too many or somebody spiked my drinks."

Without Jos the Cougars went down to a 93-nil defeat (see sports pages for match report)

COLDSTONE JOURNAL February 2nd 1976

Mr and Mrs J Sleight are pleased to announce the birth of a daughter,

Josephine Elspeth on January 28th at The Oaks Maternity Home.

DAILY COMET November 14th 1980

Rugby Star's Father Killed

The father of Coldstone's star winger, Jos Sleight was killed in an accident at the junction of Manchester Road and Factory Lane last night. Mr Sleight was crossing the road when he was struck by a car driven by a Mr James Handy. Mr Sleight Senior was rushed to hospital but never regained consciousness and died shortly after. The coroner has been informed.

COLDSTONE JOURNAL November 18th 1980

Sleight ,Josiah David on 13th November in Coldstone General Hospital after a tragic accident. Funeral on 23rd November at St Swithin's Church at 11.30 and afterwards at the Colliers Rest.

DAILY COMET January 12th 1981

TRAGIC MISJUDGEMENT LED TO DEATH

A verdict of accidental death was recorded on Mr Josiah Sleight, father of rugby star Jos Sleight. Mr Sleight was killed while crossing the road after leaving the Colliers Rest public house in Factory Lane. Witnesses stated that the traffic lights at the junction of Manchester Road were green when Mr Sleight crossed the road. He obviously misjudged the speed of the oncoming car driven by Mr James Handy.

The coroner stated that though Mr Sleight had been drinking, post-mortem tests had shown that his blood-alcohol level was quite low. He was in no way inebriated. He had simply made an error of judgement. No blame should be attached to the driver of the vehicle involved, Mr James Handy. He had no time to brake when Mr Sleight stepped in front of him.

Mr Handy was in fact an acquaintance of the Sleight family. His father had been the milkman who actually delivered Jos Sleight when the latter's mother had gone into premature labour. "My father is a friend of the family. He's devastated at what has happened," stated James.

COLSTONE JOURNAL February 14th 1981

Handy - Sleight The marriage took place at Coldstone Registry Office between Mr Timothy Handy and Mrs J. Sleight (widow) on February 12th. Honeymoon in Skegness.

MOTHER'S DAY

Mother's day is coming up
Don't buy me any 'goodies'
Like gold and beads and jewellery
They might attract the 'hoodies'.

I've body butter, shower jel
And nick-nacks in galore.
Then lots of lovely ornaments,
Who could ask for more?

I've gloves and scarves and handbags,
And every type of hat.
The perfumes I've had bought me,
Would outdo a wild pole-cat.

So get me a 'fella' off Facebook,
I don't mind if he's past his prime.
One with a car and some spirit,
Don't tell him I'm seventy nine.

I know that you like to buy flowers
And chocs or a piece of nice 'bling',
I still do respect your Dad's memory,
But I just want to have a last fling.

NIAGARA FALLS

A spectacular sight
from the Canadian side.
But the best place of all
for a view of the falls –
is to sail on the Maid of the Mist.

Over the horseshoe shape
to the rocks below us
the blue water rushes,
it sprays – it gushes,
then into the river it flows.

Our battle with the capes,
kites rising in the air.
Against the wind we fought
to keep us dry, we thought,
blue plastic stuck to clothes and hair.

Ship's running commentary –
drowned sound mid mighty roars.
'Welcome to Niagara Falls'
a Captain proudly calls
as amateur sailor's laughter soars.

I captured a moment with a click,
A special memory encased.
Against this magnificence
I felt so insignificant
and the presence of God's grace.

A CHRISTMAS STORY – MYRA

Myra had never felt so lonely. This was going to be her first Christmas without her partner Henry who had sadly died. She had had to move to a smaller place. It was going to be totally different to last Christmas when she had been surrounded by her big family and the children had loved her. She knew that the best way to get rid of her loneliness was to sleep – but she wasn't really tired.

She stood outside by the wall and leaned on the gate with her head down. Suddenly, a little girl with twinkling blue eyes and blonde curls ran up to her. Myra recognized her as one of the children who lived in the house on the corner.

"Will you be in our play?" she shouted excitedly. Her mum caught up with her. "The school is doing the nativity play in a different way this year," she said. "Parents and friends are included as well as the children, so we wondered if you would like to join us. You'll soon get used to everyone. I'll sort out the ins and outs and take you along. We've known you a few weeks now and the way you look and walk is a great advantage. You'll be so good".

Myra couldn't believe her luck. She had been on stage before, many years ago, and knew she had a gift for this sort of thing. Her looks and her demeanour hadn't changed. She'd do a good job.

The night of the play arrived and she waited patiently in the wings. Everyone else was excited and tense but she was calm and quiet.

"You'll be the star of the show" said the young man playing Joseph as he leaned on her shoulder.

"Hope I'm not too heavy" said the girl playing Mary as she climbed on her back.

Myra the donkey moved forward to gasps from the audience and then applause. Of course baby Jesus was the star but *she* carried the mother of the star, and in so doing would enjoy the happiest of Christmases.

She brayed with delight.

COLOUR PREJUDICE

In a sanctuary at Formby,
A small red squirrel plays.
He's watched and fed with loving care
By folk who love his ways.

He knows he's special 'cause he's rare
And easy on the eye.
Enthusiasts make careful notes,
His species mustn't die.

In a small back garden here in Leigh,
Another squirrel calls.
It's nice to see him jump the fence,
Climb up and down the walls.

But others have tried to chase him out.
He's deemed a threat they say.
The traps will get him, then he'll die,
And that's because he's grey.

SPRING

Spring is here, summer's near
Come along my little dear
Dance with me over the meadows
Together we'll skip
Over the rivers and streams
Fly over the valleys and mountains
Race with the golden eagles
High amongst the clouds

We'll use the wind for our sails
Fast flowing currents for speed
Run through the plateaus and forests
And when we see a pregnant deer
Springing down the narrow path
We'll follow her tracks

When witnessing her little fawn
Coming into this world
We stop for a moment
To rejoice nature's miracle
And to welcome the arrival
Of a new life
And a fresh, new spring

Chase away dark clouds
Invite radiant star
Rejoice the sunrise
Bid the sunset goodnight
Live for today
For tomorrow will remain a mystery

MY BEAUTIFUL SUNFLOWER

A bird dropped a sunflower seed in my back garden. I only knew about it when I saw it sprouting by the brick wall. It grew in leaps and bounds. I looked after it and fed it once a day with a special fertilizer. When its stem outgrew me, I tied it to an eight foot stake and waited impatiently for it to open its face. One summer's day, as I looked out through my kitchen window I saw it blooming. I ran outside to take a closer look. Wow! Its round face framed by golden petals beamed down at me. I smiled, happy to see its glowing face. My sunflower was the tallest flower in my garden. My neighbours loved its radiant face peeping at them over the wall. We took many photographs posing by its side, our faces beaming with happy smiles. The birds were also attracted to its round, perfect face and visited my sunflower day after day. They sat on its freckled face, testing its offspring and when they were ripe and ready to eat, they picked out its tasty seeds.

One Sunday morning as the church bells rang. I walked up my garden path and stopped in front of my pride and joy. Its once beautiful face was full of holes and its golden crown was losing its glow. The summer was coming to an end, so was the short life span of my sunflower. Its leaves started to brown and sag. I touched its stalk and looked into its scarred, sad face. Some of the seeds were hiding under the curly rim of its floppy hat. We gazed at each other from different heights. Its droopy head swayed in the breeze and I am sure I heard it whispering; saying how happy it was growing in my cottage garden. Thanking me for all my loving care and attention, telling me that she'd managed to save some of her offspring, especially for me.

Another summer gone, another year lost never to return. And as I pulled out the seedlings I said, "When dark nights are here again and when I feel sad and lonely, I'll look at the photographs I took of you. Your sunny face and your golden smile will brighten up my winter's days. And in the spring I'll plant your offspring by the wall in my back garden and watch them grow."

HORSES FOR COURSES

Horses are fed a wholesome diet
Grass, cereals and hay.
Much the same as cattle eat
How can we say neigh?

Protein rich and full of iron,
Horse-beef is nutritious.
Cooked in various recipes,
It can be quite delicious.

Many European butchers
Sell horse meat every day.
It's set out in the window
As part of the display.

The population's growing fast
We cannot be too fussy.
So put some horse-beef in the pan
And put some on your 'butty'.

It may just need more cooking
'Cos it might have run the course.
So get your blinking blinkers off
There's nothing wrong with horse.

COLD COMFORT

Joe Kelly was mad, mad, mad, not insane just furious.

'How could they leave him out of the team?'

The fifteen year old didn't see the beauty of the field covered in un-trodden snow. Reaching the end of the lane he took a mighty kick at a snowball realizing too late it was a snow covered stone. It jarred his foot sending pain shooting up his leg. It fuelled an already blazing temper. Joe turned unto the High Street and limped to the delicatessen. Inside the shop a bespectacled policeman lifted a cup of coffee from the counter. He held a plate of spaghetti in his other hand. Two members of the team stood before the counter. Joe knew they had seen him by their sly grins. Two freshly made Vanilla milkshakes were placed before the boys; it was too much! Joe took a deep breath and blew the froth off the drinks into the unfortunate policeman's spectacles completely blinding him. The plate tilted.

Spaghetti slid off the plate onto the head of a diner. It covered his bald pate with white curls, the long strings dangling over his ears changing him instantly into a high court judge.

Joe fled, missing a grotesque ballet, danced by his three victims, striving to keep their feet on tiles covered by vanilla milk foam and spaghetti.

LAND OF HOPE

Betsey Smith and Alice Booth lived in two of the stone cottages that were all that was left of the Hamlet of Byrneside. The market town of Marsland had spread over the moors, building many new houses to cope with the overspill.

The two friends sat in Betsey's kitchen discussing the imminent arrival of the new tenants, rumoured to be refugees or immigrants.

'What will happen?' Alice asked her friend.

Betsey thought before answering.'My Grandfather told me a story he heard during the war.'

'Two men met in a bar. 'Do you like Americans?' one asked. 'No' was the reply. 'Do you like the French?' 'No' was the answer. 'Ah, you just like the English.' Again the answer was 'No'.

Puzzled, the man asked, 'Don't you like anyone?'

'Yes.' He was told. 'I like my friends.'

Betsey looked at her friend, 'We have always been good neighbours, we must try to carry on.'

The next day Betsey was startled by her little son's noisy arrival home. She could see he was bursting with excitement.

'Whatever is the matter, Daniel?' she asked.

Daniel pointed toward the house next door. He managed to say one word, 'Friend'.

His mother understood. Daniel had never had a playmate his own age. Shedding her apron, patting her hair into place, she took hold of her son's hand. Together they went into the garden.

A stone wall separated them from the next house. A boy of Daniel's age a little taller and thinner than her son, stood on the other side of the wall. His face was the colour of milk chocolate, his hair tight black curls. Before Betsey could speak, Daniel called out, 'I'm your friend Daniel.'

'Tell Daniel your name!'. A beautiful young woman with the carriage of a queen spoke softly to her son.

'I am Gabriel.' The boy reached up shyly and touched Daniel's hand. It began a friendship which was to strengthen as time passed. The parents exchanged greetings and names.

Soon, the Nigerian and English families were comfortable neighbours. Together they watched with interest as the former village grew. As more people moved into Byrneside, they watched it change. Not only the council houses filled with tenants, but some of the stone buildings were reclaimed taking on a new lease of life. The old stone barn became a mixed grocery and newsagents owned by an Asian family. Another barn was extended and modernised to make a Chinese chip shop. The old inn took on new life as a modern hotel. Some adults got together and decided to rebuild the bombed out chapel to make a meeting place. There were many volunteers to help; soon they had a community centre of which they could be justly proud. They called it Hope Hall.

Jan Kowalski, a young sportsman retired through injury, undertook to be a youth leader. At the grand opening of the centre, Jan stood with Betsey, looking at the many nationalities brought together.

'When I had my first class' he said 'I asked myself how would I cope with so many different cultures and languages. The children gazed up at me, all different except for their expressions. The faces carried the same look of expectation and hope.'

'It's what we all have in common; hope and love,' Betsey said, her eyes on Daniel and Gabriel and their friends.

This is a new beginning, the children will lead the way, we older ones must learn from them.

FROG

A frog with a tongue,
A long, long tongue,
Long and sticky and fast and strong,
Sitting by a pond
For its dinner one day,
Hoping for a fly to pass that way,
Ah!! ....
Long and sticky and fast and strong
Aaaaaah .... fly ....good .....b-y-e.

JANUARY

A winter wonderland of ice and snow
Produced by nature through the long dark night
The children play, their faces all aglow

Brave sledgers speed as fast as they can go
And young lads making snowballs for a fight
A winter wonderland of ice and snow

Although a cold wind from the north does blow
And Jack Frost's icy chill at fingers bite
The children play, their faces all aglow

White branches on the hedgerows make a show
The berries standing out so red and bright
A winter wonderland of ice and snow

A snowman in the corner starts to grow
He's finished off with hat and scarf wrapped tight
The children play, their faces all aglow

The sun turns red and starts to dip below
A scene to fill all hearts with such delight
A winter wonderland of ice and snow
The children play, their faces all aglow

TYLDESLEY PARISH CHURCH

It stands atop a hill, overlooking three towns, Tyldesley, Atherton and Leigh.
The plains of Cheshire and Jodrell Bank are sights that you can see.
Pennine Chain, Rivington Pike also the hills of Wales.
As you look around, there's Derbyshire, with its Peaks and with its Dales.
The tower was unsafe so the bells couldn't ring, but the vergers came up with an idea.
Donations not gifts for their Ruby Wedding, for electronic bells to ring clear.
The bells now installed ring out every Sunday, for special occasions as well.
And the congregation, and people around, rejoice at the sound of the bell.

THE FRIGHT OF MY LIFE

My heart pounded and my legs turned to jelly. What was that noise? Was it footsteps or someone breathing heavily? I stopped, listened intently. No, it was just my imagination.

I had started to walk on when I heard it again, it was definitely footsteps. There wasn't a light to be seen, nowhere to run to, no-one to ask for help. I could feel the sweat running down my back as I hurried, my breath rasping in the cold air.

What was I to do? Get out of here as quickly as I could was my next thought and I started to run. As I ran, the eerie footsteps quickened. Whoever it was, was following me. Gasping with every step I ran faster until I could see lights in the near distance.

As I neared the lighted street, I realised that the footsteps had stopped, and when I looked back I instantly knew why. I had been running down a tunnel and my pursuant had been the echo from my footsteps.

DIET

Of late, I have put on weight,
So, decided to halve my plate.
Crack. Crick. Plate's split. Dunnit!

THE FLORIST

She stood admiring the display of flowers,
Carnations, parrot tulips and deep red roses
Gypsophelia and maiden hair fern
Arranged into bouquets and posies

Across the room in bowls and vases
Chrysanthemums, lillies and iris abound
Bracken and lilac spill out of the bowls
Leaves resting on the ground

A bridal bouquet is in the making
Cream roses to match the bride's gown
Tear drops of dew glistening on the roses
Making a jewel in the crown

Holly, fern and leaves from shrubs
Go into bouquet making
Chrysanthemums, fresia and also carnations
Are flowers just for the taking

The bouquet complete, and the weight off her feet
No reason for her to complain
She sits in a chair and takes off her shoes
And forgets that her feet are in pain

JOINING THE W.I.

Jam and Jerusalem was the cry,
When my sons learned that I'd joined the W.I.
We did sing Jerusalem at every meeting
But no signs of Jam t'was biscuits we were eating.

Our Branch had a craft group which I joined eagerly.
Where I found that my talents were most meagerly.
We'd a lady who made quilted bedspreads,
Stitched by hand with long silken threads.

Another spun wool from which she wove cloth.
And one made up recipes for soup and for broth.
I soon learned to quilt and make pictures in cross stitch,
And cards made with silk in colours so rich.

We had fairs where we sold the things we had made,
Including some jam which was AA+ grade.
We had lots of ideas for raising some money,
But not a “Calendar”, we didn't find that funny.

DREAMING

I remember a garden but don't know where.
It must have been springtime because tulips grew there.
There was also a blossom filled apple tree,
And a door in a wall for which I had the key.
There was a small lake and rippling stream,
When the sun caught the ripples they started to gleam.
A small wooden bridge ran over the water,
The sound of children filled the air with laughter.
I turned a corner and guess what I found,
Swings and slides in a children's playground.
Families with children were picnicking there,
And there in the shadows a girl with blond hair.
She was standing watching beneath an oak tree,
And when I approached I saw it was me.
I was back in my childhood with my Aunty May,
At Walkden Park where she took us to play.
My dream became jumbled, Barrow Bridge, Moss Bank Park,
I awoke with a start to the song of a lark

VILLANELLE – CONFLICT

I look back over a most horrendous year
Darkness enfolding, no gleam of a light
Disaster for those whom some hold most dear.

Sickness, poverty what more can they fear.
No one caring about their sad plight.
I look back over a most horrendous year..

Children dying with no close family near
Why are these innocents involved in fight?
Disaster for those whom some hold most dear.

Bystanders doing nothing else but jeer.
Not helping the wounded that are in sight.
I look back over a most horrendous year.

Soldiers decked out in their camouflaged gear.
Snipers firing through day and through the night
Disaster for those whom some hold most dear.

No sign of a cease fire or an all clear
This bloody carnage cannot be alright.
I look back over a most horrendous year,
Disaster for those whom some hold most dear.

ETERNAL LOVE

A pair of swans were
Courting on the lake
Their elegant necks swaying
Their beautiful wings arching
Two perfect hearts reflecting
Sailing through the sky

They glided majestically
Over the glossy surface
Their supple necks entwined
In a loving embrace, high and low
Amongst the fluffy clouds
And dancing ripples

The cob and his beautiful pen
Swam gracefully
'Prince and Princess' of the lake
They didn't need marital vows
Church bells or a wedding party
They had each other's eternal love

They were happy flying
Happy swimming side by side
Displaying their eternal devotion
For all to envy
By waltzing around the lake
Proudly and gracefully

When noticing my presence
They swam towards the grassy bank

The Magic of Words

Bowing their royal heads
Before me, I felt privileged and
Acknowledged their greetings
With a smile and equal affection

After sharing my lunch
With a love bonding pair
I watched them swimming away
In their wake, they left
Their famous Victorious signs
For me to read and to cherish
Vowels of eVerlasting loVe

CATSLEEPER

Little curled up cat,
With your nose tucked in.
We can't see your chin
While you're sleepin'.

With your tail curled round,
And your purring sound,
Safe and warm.

WIGAN REVISITED

In factories and mines our forebears worked in cloth and coal,
They were glad to be employed instead of on the dole.
Each worker came home tired, but satisfied, a job well done.
Then the annual trip to Blackpool where the family had their fun.

The area has been transformed for happiness and health,
Go to Leigh flash and feed the ducks, then picnic there yourself.
There are lots of folk enjoying our woodlands and green spaces,
One doesn't need to go abroad to those exotic places.

Take a walk along the towpath in the Wigan Greenheart Park,
You may see hares and rabbits and a woodpecker or lark.
The waters sustain roach and perch and give anglers much pleasure,
Long boats pass by with families enjoying aquatic leisure.

Go to the southern side of Leigh to join the River Glaze,
Stroll through the woods at Windy Bank and see skylarks and jays.
Occasionally a roe deer, then perhaps a stoat or weasel,
So everyone enjoy yourselves, and artists take your easel.

PIT DISASTER

In the past local miners and pitmen endured relentless hardship and danger as they worked the mines. This poem was written in 2010, to commemorate the Centenary of the Pretoria Pit Disaster in Westhoughton in 1910. A number of Tyldesley miners were among those who lost their lives:

Deep, in the pit

They worked to get,

Coal from the earth, through toil and sweat,

Through toil and sweat.

These colliers took it in their stride,

Risked danger daily, in dark and grime,

In dark and grime.

The same each day,

For just small pay,

They hacked and laboured -- come what may,

Come what may.

These colliers took it in their stride,

Risked danger, daily, in dark and grime,

In dark and grime.

Came this cruel, crushing date,

Three hundred and forty four faced their fate,

They faced their fate.

Their lives were lost.

Almighty Blast!

Took these brave men,

Who breathed their last,

They breathed their last.

These colliers took it in their stride,

Risked danger daily in dark and grime,

In dark and grime.

Deep in the pit,

They worked to get, their mates

From the earth, through toil and sweat,

Their toil and sweat

WERE YOU THERE?

We were –
my sister and I.
We were there at the unveiling.
We bathed in the winter sun,
shining bright, reflecting the glistening
light off the chain of office
around Mayor Brian Clare's chest.
A chest that within
beat a heart
full of pride as his
lifetime's ambition
came to fruition.
We heard his words
and saw the trees
in Ditchfield Park
as they swayed in the breeze,
shedding snow
onto the onlookers,
sugaring them like seasonal mince pies
as Wingates band played
'The Dead March in Saul'
with tears in their eyes.
We stamped our feet
in tune with the beat,
to keep warm as we stood
on a carpet
of snow and ice.
We heard the sighs at the sight
when the black cloth was drawn
reverently away from the monument.

Jane Robins' sculpture,
revealing a bronze miner
kneeling in reflection and meditation.
There forever in remembrance of deceased
whose names are etched deep
in the granite behind him.
He has downed his pitman's tools,
the pick he used
to dig for the Hulton coal.
Fuels from fossilised treasure
mined from a great black hole
that blew in December 1910
killing 344 boys and men.
And, as the lightest of snow fell
and the hell of Westhoughton's darkest day
was remembered, we wept.

METAPHORS (AND OTHERS)

When I opened Mary's email and saw that we had to write about metaphors, I felt sick as a parrot. Trying to differentiate between a simile, a metaphor and even an allegory has frequently proved difficult for me. I eventually understood the simile. Like riding a bike, once mastered never forgotten, but the thought of metaphors brings on the same feeling of horror I got on the day I was handed a logarithm book at school – it's all Greek to me.

When the panic brought on by the email subsided, I remembered that I know a man who can help – Mr. William Shakespeare. In his plays he throws out metaphors like confetti at a wedding. He has written a play about a student named Hamlet who returns home from university to find his country, Denmark, in a bit of a mess. Metaphorically, it is an `unweeded garden'. (Mr. Shakespeare likes his unweeded gardens, as we shall see.) But Hamlet has more problems to worry about than the `rotten' state of Denmark. He is told that his father has died, his mother has married his Uncle Claudius, who is now king, and that they didn't even save him a piece of cake. It is not difficult to sympathise with the mourning Hamlet, when he is told by his mother to stop behaving like a spoiled child because `everybody dies`; or when he starts to show signs of becoming as mad as a hatter and sees a ghost clanking around the castle walls at midnight. From personal experience I know that the majority of students go home at the end of term and turn their parents' house into a rubbish tip, but the grieving Hamlet forgoes the pleasures of leaving his clothes on the bedroom floor and instead starts to talk to himself about the pros and cons of committing suicide (Mr. Shakespeare calls this a soliloquy). `To be or not to be,' ponders Hamlet. This is where I start to lose a bit of patience. Most people, having had a day like Hamlet, would simply say that they have had `a bad day at the office'. Not Hamlet. He has to confuse me by talking of `the slings and arrows of outrageous fortune', and the `whips and scorns of time'. But there is a light at the end of this particular tunnel. As I am wrestling with the meanings of this speech another part of my brain is telling me to forget it, that I am not yet half way into the play (a very long play) and there will be many more lengthy speeches with metaphors (and allegories and imagery) to contemplate. There is no chance of saying `Good night, sweet prince' to Hamlet yet. This is unfortunate for the majority of the other characters in the play because Hamlet's quest for revenge cuts short their chance to speak in riddles – I mean metaphors.

This play is one of Mr. Shakespeare's tragedies, so nearly everybody dies. Eventually it is Uncle Claudius' turn to kick the bucket and Hamlet manages to get the last word in before the king is as dead as a doornail. Claudius, once a mere weed, has flowered into an `incestuous, murd'rus, damned Dane'. At last Hamlet has managed a metaphor that is short, sweet and makes sense. I would say short, sweet and to the point, but as Hamlet has just been stabbed it might be seen as a pun and I don't want to open that particular can of worms.

I like *Hamlet*, I have read/seen it a few times, and have mostly managed to get through it without worrying too much about the more oblique metaphors – there are plenty of other things in the play to exercise the old grey matter. I also like Mr. Shakespeare's *Richard II*. Although he is described by the metaphors `lion' and `sun', Richard is really not very good at the job of being king. He, too, has an uncle, one John of Gaunt, who he thinks is a pain in the whatsit, or a `lunatic lean-witted fool'. Happily for Richard, Uncle John dies quite early in the play, but not without warning Richard that he wouldn't be getting many votes if he was on a talent show. In one of Mr. Shakespeare's most famous speeches, Uncle John reminds Richard that as monarch he is custodian of England, which he describes, amongst many glorious metaphors, as a `sceptred isle' a `precious stone set in a silver sea', an `Eden, demi paradise'. He may be laying it on a bit thick, but I am a patriot and I understand and entirely agree with what he is saying. However, Richard takes no notice of these words of wisdom (maybe because he isn't on stage when the speech is made). He just carries on stealing land, imposing taxes and generally enjoying being a clever Richard.

As our `lion' continues on his path of self-destruction, Mr. Shakespeare introduces a scene where, unusually for him, he tells the story from the point of view of two commoners, Richard's gardeners. They view England as a land full of weeds, choked flowers and unpruned trees, all the fault of

Richard, who is no longer a `lion' but a `wasteful king'. I think that it is very sensible of the gardeners to talk in metaphors. If they said what they really meant they would probably be arrested for treason and I have read that life in the Tower of London in those days was not exactly a bed of roses. This whole garden scene is an extended metaphor, or an allegory of England (I read that on the Internet), but I don't want to open that particular can of worms.

I like the fact that Mr. Shakespeare keeps this scene simple. He tells us what is happening to Richard and to the country without over-complicating the language. Maybe I have the Idiot's Guide copy of this play, but I find its metaphors easier to understand than those in *Hamlet*. In comparison, it is like manna from heaven – but that's another simile.

LONGING FOR OUTDOORS

To see the trees for real,
Not watch them through the window.
To hear the breeze brush through the bushes,
And feel the rippling waves of leaves.
To smell the new cut grass,
And know the twilight dropping.
The sudden flap of the nest-bound bird.
The after-freshness of rain on the wind,
Real, not through the window.

NINE AND A HALF LIVES (A VERY TRUE STORY)

It had snowed quite quietly whilst we were watching TV. It was Friday night with a busy weekend ahead. Sandy the big bold ginger tom was wailing to be let out by the back door.
"OK but back quick, it's snowed out there and your paws will get frozen!"
Horlicks made, TV switched off, only the cat to be let in..............
but no Sandy yet and it's after midnight now, I'll just have my drink and try again in a while.
Nothing doing yet again, he'll just have to stay out the night. Let's lock up.
He's a resourceful cat, been in many a scrape, so he'll be OK, no doubt be scratching at the door first thing.

More snow overnight, no sign of Sandy, bright sharp blue skies next morning.
No sign all day, maybe back tomorrow, he's never gone for this long!!!
Sunday turned to Monday, Tuesday and Wednesday, time to ask around and knock on doors, check all the usual haunts, garages, sheds and hidey holes..... no nothing, no sign anywhere.

Days turned to weeks, he's gone for good, distressed and lost in the snow. The snow turns to slush, the slush melts away and still no sign of Sandy.

Always looking out, always that chance, two, three weeks gone by now.

Week Four…….cat bed washed and fluffed up……. just in case.
Week Five……..gave tins of Whiskers and pilchards to friends who had cats.

Week Six……….no news at all.

Week Seven …..dishes and bowls went the same way as the food.

Week Eight………
Basket and carrying igloo dropped off for Cats' Protection League.

Week Nine……….
"I thought I saw Sandy sneaking along the wall by the school when I drove past, I even stopped and had a good walk around."
"No never, not now, I think we have to face facts, it's been too long"

Week Ten………..
Called to post a letter on the way home from work, turned the corner to our house and who should spring up out of the garden at number 47 but Sandy, bedraggled and thin, very much worse for wear, he padded along home beside me like it was only yesterday!

CAPUT

You've cracked the icing,
You've shattered the dream.
You've gone off with her,
Your wife's your has-been.

She'd have you back,
You bet she would,
To see you and hold you,
And call you Love.

But it's gone like rainbows,
That fade 'ere you know.
The door has been closed now.
The bridge's been blown.
She's left there weeping by water's side,
Flung out of the lifeboat, on the ebb tide.

You've done it, you've wrecked it,
The trust is gone.
It's so fundamental.
The knell is knolled.

You're not what she thought.
You're not who she knew.
She's grieving, 'n' hurting,
Can this be you?

It is. It's all shattered.
Can never come back.
She wants to hate you,
Can't even do that.

RIVINGTON AUTUMN

The heather blooming dully,
At Summer's end,
To no breeze bends.

The wind rushing,
Reddens our faces,
To match the Autumn leaves.
We can see them far below,
Rusting on the trees.

The faded grasses grown quite yellow,
Obediently sway,
This way and that,
Willed by the wind,
Until we press them,
With our feet,
And leave them flat.
Ready for the snow,
Awaiting its hour in patience,
To wrap the hills and plants

In cold, season's white,
And bed them down for Winter.

PHOTOS

We used to want the photos out.
Reluctant she'd agree.
Lift them off the cupboard top in their old leather bag,
Some quite brown and faded,
Showing folks of her young day,
Dressed in their yesterday clothes.
"This was your Grandad."
"Where are you Mum?"
Dingy streets and pokey houses.
Set faces, barely smiling.
"This is Uncle Jim.
He was fine and tall.
Went down on a minesweeper,
In the Second World War.
His baby son just born.
That's him, your cousin Philip.
Jim never got the news."
She looks down.
Hint of a frown.
Puts it back in the bag.
"Never join the Navy, son," she says.

SATURDAY MORNINGS

On Saturday mornings,
Queuing down the steps and round the corner,
Impatient for the doors to open and then,
Moving forward, shuffle by shuffle,
The ticket pumped out at the desk.

Ushers in uniforms
And everywhere seems bright and clean,
Or is it the projected gleam of our excited anticipation,
Of what is to come?

Sitting on a long padded seat, playing by pressing the keys
And swinging his legs and feet down onto the treddles,
Driving this musical monster, is the organist.
Rising up from somewhere below, like something from Jules Verne,
But without the seaweed and water.
The lord of all bright lights and knobs and mother-of-pearl,
He lodges the organ into its predetermined spot, where we can see as well as hear him.
As the curtains draw back, rich red and golden-brocade edged, he plays
Up and up to a grand crashing crescendo ....Daa, Daa, Da, Daaa ......
And all us kids are shouting for what is getting closer ......the Show.

But first it's songs. Words on the screen, with a bouncing ball, boynging from word to word,
To show us where we're up to. So, we "Keep right on to the end of the road" and
"Pack up our troubles in our old kit bag" and try to sing of Bluebirds and the White Cliffs of Dover.

The commissionaire, in maroon double-breasted greatcoat, padded shoulder, epaulettes, brass buttons
And peaked matching cap on his head, affirms his authority.

Just to ensure we know who is in charge, he walks hard, up and down the central aisle, bawling,
"No chuckin' orange peel."
"No chuckin' lolly sticks."
"No messin', or yer out on yer ear..."
The voice and grammar not quite living up to the regal uniform.
And despite a whispered, "Little Hitler", we all get the message.
Any daredevil or would-be-rebel is clocked by the hawk-eyes and hauled out.

The lights go down and we settle for Pearl and Dean adverts and that ebullient cockerel,
Screeching and Crowing with all his might from his perch on high,
Even outdoing the fanfare of rousing music, proclaiming the

imminence of Pathe News.
The mood lifts for cartoons and Laurel and Hardy, Old Mother Riley, The Three Stooges and Mr. Pastry.
Even though we don't like them all, our laughing and oohing and aahing, carry us through to
Lights-up and the interval, which we hate, partly because of the disruption to our enjoyment, but mostly because, the ice creams, lollies and popcorn are beyond our budget, but our misery is short.

Dimming lighting is simultaneous with the best part starting. Immediately, we are embroiled in a life of thrills, fears, disbelief, worries, hopes, skullduggery and heroism, as we are heart-and-soul at one with the Lone Ranger, hordes of Cowboys and Indians and ….. Flash Gordon!! Galloping on horses, firing six-shooters, looking over our shoulders for the enemy, believing always in Lassie and in the extreme far-offness of deep space, marvelling at gleaming spaceships and amazing attire.

We are in a frenzy of cheering, clapping, jumping up and down, willing the Goodies to escape, vanquish, outride, outrun, outshoot, outfly, outwit the Baddies ….. to whom we direct everything we can, short of physically leaping into the film itself, by booing, roaring and bumping our feet, to bring about their demise. A whole Picture House full of kids, stomping and stamping in unison, drowning out the sound track of horses' hooves, hollering cowboys, gunshots, whoops of Red Indians

.... and the dictats of Ming the Merciless. Boys have little fights in the seats sometimes, as if the excitement on the screen has burst out and radiated into them.

All these 1950s kids, mostly in hand-me-down, homemade and make-do clothes, are unlikely little anarchists and, in an instant, can be chilled into silent awe, at the dire plights their heroes get mired in.

The more of the films we see, the more we want them to go on, pouring into our brains through our eyes and ears, flooding our imaginations and carting the lot of us off to where we love to be.

While we're still hot in the chase, or relieved to have evaded capture .... without warning ... it's all over. The Baddies lose. The Goodies win. Justice is done, except for Flash Gordon, still in the dread clutches of Ming. The only way to allay our anxiety for him, is to 'COME BACK NEXT WEEK'. Overheated, dazed, our cheeks flushed, we totter outside, blinking into the light of day like newborn kittens.

SHORT DAYS

White hoar frost
Overlays the fallen snow,
Sparkling, crisp, sugar-looking dust.
Crept already into trees, the trunks and branches and left-over leaves,
And grasses too, who've valiantly clung by half dead roots to the earth.
Insidious invader.
Bushes limp and frozen down,
Resigned, surrendered,
In captive bonds to Winter.
Moon is still out,
Tho' daytime's here.
Doing overtime reluctantly,
"No joy in this for me."
Half there and miserably,
Wants to go home and leave it to the shirking Sun,
Barely there, a weakly orb,
Subdued, held on the horizon,
In a pink-edged sky.

THE IDEAL CHILD

I make Mum's breakfast every day
Rub up Dad's shoes at night.
I dust and hoover regularly
And clean the windows bright.

I do the washing every week,
Clear all the ironing too.
Then once my homework's finished off,
I even clean the loo.

I'm good at sport; good looking too.
At school I'm always top.
I'm so polite; I'm seen, not heard,
My standards never drop.

My parents are so proud of me,
I'm all that they desire.
Oh, one thing I forgot to say –
I'm a huge compulsive liar !!

EASTER

As Easter day dawned, and Emma sleepily made her Mum a cup of tea, she knew that today was going to be truly memorable. England, 1946. The first Easter after the war. It was her special birthday, and Mum's too. They would share this milestone together. Emma had been born on Mum's 20th birthday and it was really fortunate that this year it fell on Easter Sunday.

People were still recovering from the ravages of war. There was rationing, austerity and poverty but for today all that would be forgotten. She couldn't wait to get to church. Three of her school friends would be there, sitting near the back in their new Easter outfits. Everyone wore new on Easter Sunday and Emma was no exception. She had saved up her clothing coupons and had splashed out on a grey coat with black patent leather trimmings on the cuffs and pockets. She had also trimmed up an old grey felt hat and had made it look like new. She would wear it at a jaunty angle to show it off.

She hoped her new beau George would be impressed. He would be there in the pew waiting for her – third row from the front. How she loved that man and he felt the same way about her. She had known him only a few months but had definitely found her soul mate. Mum usually accompanied her to church but had decided not to come today. Emma had a strong Christian ethic and loved church. She would savour this day for ever.

Meanwhile, back at home and unknown to Emma, Leah (her Mum) was being picked up and chauffeured to the church hall by Mrs. Walker, the president of the Mothers Union. The committee had been very helpful to Leah since she had been widowed and had gone out of its way to ensure that she and Emma were never lacking in support or friendship.

Leah had always dreamt of Emma finding a boyfriend, becoming independent of her and settling down. Now, at last, it seemed that her dream would materialise. George was a lovely man and she would have bagged him for herself had she been a few years younger! She knew she didn't look her age.

Age was just a number and she knew she was still attractive, mainly because of her personality.

Today was a milestone for both of them and they would go onwards and upwards, albeit separate ways. She mustn't be sad. She wasn't losing a daughter but gaining a son – and a handsome one at that! Anyway, they would probably have to live with her as houses were scarce in these difficult post war times.

When the service finished, Emma and George were taken aside by the vicar as the congregation filed past them and into the church hall. After a certain amount of small talk, the vicar ushered them through the door. Immediately there were cheers of 'Happy Birthday!' from the assembled company.

"Mum, you're here!" cried Emma, looking at the smart little lady sitting by a table which held a large birthday cake and an even larger card – both home-made and both perfect. She was surrounded by spam sandwiches, jellies, blancmanges and loads of other little goodies which people must have saved up their food points to get.

"Very, very special happy birthday again, Mum! This is a lovely surprise for both of us."

"Happy birthday again to you, love. I hope they give you a party as good as this when you reach your century."

"That's a long way off yet, Mum. I'm only eighty. George and I have a lot of life to plan before I catch up with you."

"Then let's eat this cake quickly. We won't get another one till your wedding!"

With that, and to the applause and cheers of the onlookers, the two old ladies laughingly hugged each other reflecting that they had lived through two world wars, yet had been blessed with long and happy lives, and were still fortunate enough to experience the most joyous of Easters.

TREASURED CHILDREN

New sounds pop from little lips and drift,
Soft as soapy bubbles floating on air.
Laughter and baby babble and short strings of words.
The camera clicks the hair, the smile, the first new tooth,
The eyes a-shine with glee.
The moment gone, the image lodged in memory.
Warm, infant skin fresh and bathed.
The stillness of the sleeping child, heavy in your arms
And the gentle rhythm of in-out breaths, that says all is ok.
No surety of future, no crystal ball.
This spark, this tiny scrap of Heaven now, is what there is.

TEA BY THE SEA

(… when everything cost a fortune and the thermos flask was a treasured thing)

It's clouded over,
But I heard Mum say,
"It can hail, rain or shine,
We're going anyway!"
A day at the sea-side,
We can hardly wait.
Bursting with excitement,
We're in such a state.

The baby's not dressed yet.
The pots'r still in the sink,
The cat is upstairs hiding.
Dad gives us a wink.
"Go outside and play, you two.
You're under our feet.
Behave yourselves, now,
The day'll be a treat."

Then he came out,
With the rucksack.
"The flask's inside, so,
Don't bang the back."
I nodded, "Yes,"
Was sure I'd heard right.

I wouldn't drop it.
I held the long strap tight.
I held it as it dangled,
Then I gave a sharp tap.
If Dad wants it banging,
It needs a good crack.
"No," shrieked my sister,
"It's going to break."
I knew by her eyes,
I'd made a mistake.

But, there was no tinkle,
Of shattered glass.
No fluid ran out,
Over the flags.
Dad opened the bag
And took out the flask.
The shiny, inner part,
Was split and smashed.

My eyes filled up,
I was that sad.
"Bang goes the tea," said he.
"Sorry Dad."
It ended up well,
For our family,
To have with the sandwiches,
We bought a sea-side jug of tea.

THE LAIR OF LIES

Where are the lies which all of us tell,
Floating round Heaven or roasting in Hell?
Are they stoking the fires for auld Nick himself?
Do they fly with the clocks from the dandelion flower?
Or cling to black clouds to drop down in a shower?
Are they nasty winged creatures that buzz round our heads,
Invading our dreams, as we sleep in our beds?
The white lies, the whoppers, the lie with a lid on,
The big fat stonkers, the scams and sting cons.
Professional lies, the ones told in fear,
Deceits, 'n' cover-ups, from those once held dear.
Do they cluster in corners, high up near the ceiling?
Sheer mendacity, wheeling and dealing?
Go steady, be easy with long feather duster,
Lest they drop from above, on your head, in a fluster.

LITTLE DRAGON

With the park to your right,
Climb steep Astley Street.
Pass where the drippy bridge had used to carry trains,
 packed full of goods and people.
With Moss View Terrace hugging the gradient,
Move left into Upper George Street.
Look up to see Dean Villa ….
Prepare now for the treat.
A terracotta dragon on the topmost gable,
Who looks as if he's able,
With a special spell,
To spring to life, stretch,
Flap his wings, take flight …. and off ….
 over the rooftops and backyards.
A quick circuit of The Square,
To swoop back to his perch,
Like an incoming swallow,
Unnoticed, unremarked, by folk below.
Is he just back from another furtive flirt around the town?
Slick scan of the street,
Sorts his wings, scales in place,
Claws re-grip the ridge.
Then, to stone once more,
'Til next time.

THE COAT

I saw my mother's old coat today as I walked down Bradshawgate. I'd know it anywhere. It was more of a mac than a coat. Dusty pink with a darker pink collar which was a bit faded at the edge. Single breasted with the top button missing. I always did mean to sew a new button on but as she rarely went out there was no point.

There's a folded rain mate in one pocket and a multi-coloured silk scarf in the other. She always felt a draught before anyone else and when she did come out in the car with me we couldn't have any windows open even on a boiling hot day with no hint of a breeze. Obviously mum wasn't wearing the coat as she's been dead since March but it was definitely hers.

I gave it to the charity shop with most of her other stuff when I cleared out the flat. Some of the clothes, the ones I'd bought her, hadn't been worn. They were still gift wrapped! She always said she was saving them for best but of course 'best' never arrived. I found five brand-new nighties and several unused Christmas presents. There was a box set of Doris Day DVD's with the cellophane still on. I bet they got a good price for those down at the charity shop.

I followed the mac lady for a bit as she browsed in Poundland and then later as she bought a ready cooked chicken from the indoor market. I stood right behind her sniffing the air to see if there was a faint smell of Coty L'aimant still clinging to the mac but there was nothing. It must have been dry cleaned. It was definitely hers.

Life's quieter now. No more looking for grocery items that don't exist or trying to find a suitable present for someone who never went out and had no hobbies except for watching TV.

On her 80th birthday mum complained bitterly when a beautiful bouquet of flowers arrived because she didn't have a vase big enough! Then she complained again after a few days when the water needed changing and they started to smell. She couldn't wait for the flowers to die so she could tell me to chuck them in the bin. I kept reviving them with fresh water and aspirin just for the hell of it.

When she did come shopping with me, long before she stopped going out, I'd whip round Sainsbury's flinging food in the trolley mentally going through the menus for a family of five for the week. Occasionally I'd catch sight of her down one of the aisles staring intently at the ingredients on a tin of soup. To be fair she was on her third set of teeth and couldn't eat anything chewy, so I always made her a large pan of cornbeef hash which I froze into individual portions. It'll be a while before I can eat cornbeef hash again. Her shopping list never varied. It was always: Slimma soup, small baked beans, small skinless boneless salmon, Horlicks, small toasty loaf, frozen cottage pie, frozen fish pie, slice of quiche (not spinach), 3 individual trifles, Maltesers, toilet roll, bottle of bleach, a TV guide and a £2 lottery lucky dip. I could have collected that food with my eyes shut. I didn't need to sit there while she pondered what to buy. Just when I thought the list was complete she would throw another three things at me as I was leaving and if I didn't get everything on that list she would look at me suspiciously like I'd forgotten something or couldn't be bothered looking for it. I spent weeks looking for

Rowntrees 'individual' trifles before being told there was "no call" for them anymore. Oh yes there is! My mother wants them! She's been eating three a week for years and now refuses point blank to have a large one and scoop out individual portions. Then there were the small jars of rindless silvershred marmalade that mysteriously disappeared overnight from the shelves of all major supermarkets and don't even get me started on talcum powder.

Of course I was too soft. I know that now. I should have been firm with her and ordered the food to be delivered once she stopped coming with me but it happened so gradually. One week we were going shopping together, then I would do the shopping using a list she'd made, then I had to make the list myself and before I knew it I was doing the whole thing from making the list to unpacking the food. She was so good at delegating she would have made an excellent manager given the right opportunity.

She had a carer called Evelyn but due to health and safety and a bad back she couldn't lift anything heavier than a teaspoon. She spent the whole time drinking tea and watching television with mum. She was invaluable.

The only piece of furniture I kept was an old display cabinet. The musty smell trapped inside was a mixture of cigar smoke and Christmases past when egg nog was drunk out of tiny sherry glasses. I threw away most of the contents in the cabinet. There was a broken Swiss Chalet weather clock made of balsa wood which had two little figures in national dress standing outside the doorway. If it was wet one of them jumped back in the chalet but I couldn't remember which one meant rain. There was a knitted Father Christmas, a small bible which was a Sunday school prize, a cup with 'World's Best Grandma' written on the front and several cheap souvenirs from holidays long gone. There was also a large collection of glasses, including six commemorating Charles and Di's wedding although she never drank alcohol. The cabinet had pride of place in the lounge. It was always locked and the small key was hidden in a vase on top.

It's funny how seeing that coat brought back lots of memories. I wonder who'll be walking around in mine when I'm gone?

SPACE HERO '61

Major Yuri Gagarin,
The first man in space.
The first Soviet cosmonaut.
Up in his capsule,
Passing and re-passing over the lands and oceans of the Earth,
Fifty years ago in 1961,
Checking and re-checking his instruments as he flew.

"He came to Brooks' Bar," I said.
Said she, "Don't be a nut!"
"He did, indeed, to visit the T.U.C,
Based in a terraced house."
The first man in space
And he came to Moss Side, Manchester.

We were let out of school,
To make our way and see
And cheer him and we did,
On a grey Manchester morning.

Standing in an open car came he,
Handsome in extreme, pristine army uniform,
And a smile to bring out the sun,
Fair finished us off.

The return to lessons after that,
The ultimate anti-climax.
Yuri Gagarin, space hero.

HEAVEN

Rugged mountains, flowing streams
Red kite soars and buzzard screams
Ravens croaking on the hill
As crows move in their young to kill

Swallows swoop, they're catching flies
Underneath the clear blue skies
A dairy farmer starts his churn
The sun is hot, I feel the burn

Spotted pecker starts to drill
A red fox slinks by water mill
Accommodation is divine
Sitting with a glass of wine

Where is this place, where all else pales?
It has to be in glorious WALES.

ODE TO MR BOYLE –
LONDON OLYMPICS OPENING CEREMONY 2012

Oh, Danny Boyle,
The folks, the folks are cheering,
Across the land and down from Manchester.
Your superb job in opening th' Olympics,
Was just so good, we watched in gobsmacked awe.

When we saw the fields turn into factories,
And heard 'Jerusalem', 'Abide with Me',
The NHS, the way we've always dreamed it,
James Bond then called upon the Monarchy.

Unfolding tale, a potted British History,
Fine tapestry of threaded act and song.
Our eyes and ears transported right there into it.
To us up North, so true, in no way wrong.

Oh, Danny Boyle,
You put us on the map again,
In style and wit,
For all the world to see.

You did it grand,
In boldness and variety,
If you were here,
We'd want to shake your hand.

TRAMP AT MY GATE

When I saw him sitting at my front gate, gazing at me pleadingly, I was overwhelmed with pity. He seemed timid and I could see fear in his sad, brown eyes but also a glimmer of hope.

'Should I let him in?' I thought whilst looking at his dirty and shabby coat. Then I noticed that he was shivering, yet it wasn't cold. I wanted to touch him, show him some affection, but I thought that I should get to know him first. He looked unhappy and hungry and was obviously homeless. I felt compassion rising within my heart. And even though I didn't know his name or his temperament I felt that I could trust him, touch him and stroke him. I opened the gate and let him sniff my hand. He wagged his tail and licked my fingers.

"Hello stranger, are you looking for a new home?"

In reply he rubbed his head against my hand and looked lovingly into my eyes.

"I take this as yes. In that case you're welcome to come in and stay with me for as long as you like."

He whimpered and wagged his tail excitedly then followed me into my kitchen.

"Well my little friend, whilst I do not know your name, I'll call you Tramp. I hope that you'll approve of it and of me and also of your new home."

Then I stroked him. Tramp barked once as if to say, 'I agree with all the rules and regulations as long as I can stay.'

"That's settled then. From now on we shall look after each other." I said whilst stroking his head, "You must be very hungry." He lifted his paw and woofed, twice, as if to say 'yes, yes.'

I shook his paw, "Pleased to meet you Tramp." Then I fed him with some left over stew. After he had eaten I took him into my back garden. His fur smelt musty so I decided to give him a bath. I brought out an old baby bath that I had in the garage and filled it with warm, soapy water. Tramp jumped inside it; he was probably used to it and enjoyed being washed. After I dried him with an old towel he lay on the lawn. The sun was high in the sky. I sat on the bench and talked to him as if I had known him for years. Tramp tilted his head to one side, pricked his ears up and listened to me attentively. I smiled, pleased to see that the fear from his eyes had vanished. “Tramp, I’m very happy that you’re not afraid any longer and glad that you’d stopped by my gate.” Tramp woofed as if he understood every word I said.

He was definitely a mongrel but that didn’t matter to me. He had a cute face, soft, floppy ears, black shiny nose and light brown, curly fur. To me he was a lovely little dog and for some strange reason, we understood each other perfectly from the moment we met.

From that day Tramp was my constant companion. He followed me around the house and the garden. When I took him for a walk he seemed quite nervous and stayed by my side. Perhaps he thought that I may leave him behind like his previous owner, who knows? Only Tramp knows but he couldn’t tell the tale. I can only guess and wonder why he ended up on the street without his collar. One thing I know for sure is that I’m very happy he chose me to be his new owner.

Each week I looked in the local paper in the lost and found column for pets, hoping that Tramp’s description wasn’t going to be in it. Luckily for me, no one ever asked for him. After some time I took him to the Vet for a check up and was glad to find that he was okay. When we got back I told him that from now on, he legally belonged to me.

He woofed and wagged his tail. He was obviously happy too, to have me as his new owner. Every time I fed him he licked my hand. In the evenings when I sat in my chair he lay by my feet, gazing at me with love and affection, as if I were his guardian angel. I looked down at him believing that Tramp was mine, sent by someone special who knew that I needed a faithful friend and companion.

GEORGIA AND THE MAGIC LAMP

When Georgia was three years old her mummy bought her a magic lamp. Every night when she went to bed the lamp was lit and she could see animals chasing each other across the ceiling of her bedroom.

She loved the giraffe best with his long spotted neck. He always came after the elephant and before the monkey who jumped up and down as he ran along.

One night Georgia was in bed watching the animals when suddenly the giraffe stopped and smiled down at her.

“Would you like a ride?”

“YES PLEASE” shouted Georgia grabbing her doggy and jumping up onto his back. She wrapped her arms around his long soft neck and laughed excitedly as he set off running to catch the elephant.

Round and round the bedroom went Georgia holding on tightly as her toys looked up in amazement.

Suddenly there was a noise on the stairs.

“STOP”, shouted Monkey. “Mummy’s coming to see if you’re asleep”.

The giraffe bent his neck and gently put Georgia back on the bed. As she snuggled down under the duvet mummy put her head around the bedroom door.

"Night, night," she said, kissing Georgia and switching off the lamp.

"Night, night, animals" whispered Georgia, smiling to herself.

DUSK

Dusk for many ages
has fallen on the earth
It hides a multitude of sins
and also things of worth
It's a kind of soothing darkness
when daylight hours go by
While man retires to dream his dreams
For some when time just flies